MAYA STONE PORTRAIT, COPÁN, HONDURAS   KENNETH GARRETT

This book is dedicated to the nine million members
of the National Geographic Society, whose support
makes possible "the increase and diffusion
of geographic knowledge."

Unlocking Secrets
of the
Unknown
WITH NATIONAL GEOGRAPHIC

Prepared by the Book Division, National Geographic Society, Washington, D.C.

Unlocking Secrets of the Unknown
WITH NATIONAL GEOGRAPHIC

PUBLISHED BY
The National Geographic Society

Gilbert M. Grosvenor, PRESIDENT AND CHAIRMAN OF THE BOARD

Michela A. English, SENIOR VICE PRESIDENT

PREPARED BY The Book Division

William R. Gray, VICE PRESIDENT AND DIRECTOR

Margery G. Dunn, Charles Kogod, ASSISTANT DIRECTORS

STAFF FOR THIS BOOK
Elizabeth L. Newhouse, MANAGING EDITOR

Thomas B. Powell III, ILLUSTRATIONS EDITOR

Lyle Rosbotham, ART DIRECTOR

Susan C. Eckert, Ann Nottingham Kelsall, RESEARCHERS

Jane H. Buxton, Barbara A. Payne, Gene S. Stuart, CONTRIBUTING EDITORS

Sandra F. Lotterman, EDITORIAL ASSISTANT

Artemis S. Lampathakis, ILLUSTRATIONS ASSISTANT

Lewis R. Bassford, PRODUCTION PROJECT MANAGER

H. Robert Morrison, Richard S. Wain, Heather Guwang, PRODUCTION

Karen F. Edwards, Elizabeth G. Jevons, Teresita Cóquia Sison, Karen Dufort Sligh, Marilyn J. Williams, STAFF ASSISTANTS

MANUFACTURING AND QUALITY MANAGEMENT

George V. White, DIRECTOR
John T. Dunn, ASSOCIATE DIRECTOR
Vincent P. Ryan, MANAGER
R. Gary Colbert

Diane L. Coleman, INDEXER

A National Geographic grant helped unearth a 2-inch, 2,000-year-old gold head—once a link of a necklace—from a royal Moche tomb near Sipán, Peru.

Preparing for takeoff, flamingos
race through shallow waters in
Africa's Great Rift Valley, where NGS
grantee M. Philip Kahl studied them.

Early Expeditions

By Leslie Allen

America's Wild West was as tame as a tearoom compared with the Chinese west of Joseph Rock's day. That, at least, was the impression the Austrian-born botanist and explorer

Joseph Rock depended upon Muli's king for safe passage through some of China's remotest areas in the 1920s.

Preceding Pages: Heavy loads and deep mud slow the going for Matthew and Marion Stirling en route to Tres Zapotes and the Olmec heartland.

gave readers of NATIONAL GEOGRAPHIC.

"I was quartered in the center of the village in a miserable old temple full of coffins," began a typical account in 1925, when "I was informed that several hundred bandits were surrounding the village and that capture was inevitable." Rock readied his .45s, motivated his men with silver coins, and, in his usual fastidious fashion, readied a supply of warm underwear, a towel, condensed milk, and chocolate for the harrowing night ahead.

Unaccountably, the bandits vanished before daybreak without firing a shot. But during two expeditions for the Society, danger never left the bullet-dodging scientist for long in the strife-torn border-

lands near Tibet. In Rock's ten GEO-GRAPHIC articles, news of uncharted peaks and unknown birds alternated with sickening accounts of slaughter and pillage, the kindness of local tribespeople with the greed and cruelty of their overlords.

Through thick and thin, Rock played the records of Enrico Caruso to his outlaw escort and bathed daily in an Aber-

Cavorting skeletons admonish spectators outside Choni's lamasery—Rock's base for two years in Gansu Province. His Autochromes illuminated countless Buddhist and shamanistic rituals.

crombie & Fitch folding bathtub. He presented the King of Muli with guns, ammunition, and news of the outside

Litter ensconces a Living Buddha crossing high grasslands in China's A'nyêmaqên range. Holy men made vital allies in war-torn hinterlands, where brigands preyed on travelers.

world; in return, the corpulent potentate exerted his influence with Tibetan bandits and made possible Rock's explorations of China's mightiest peaks, thought to be the first by a Westerner.

Rock's style was eccentric, but his sense of mission had forged the National Geographic Society itself 35 years earlier. Many of the 33 founders were themselves risk-takers driven by a quest for knowledge. The geologist John Wesley Powell had led the first Colorado River expedition 900 miles through the Grand Canyon. Russologist George Kennan had crossed Siberia by sleigh. There was Brig. Gen. Adolphus W. Greely, whose Arctic voyage had set a record for "farthest north," and George W. Melville, whose relief ship rescued Greely after three years.

President and Editor Melville Bell Grosvenor, not yet born at the Society's inception in 1888, looked back on the founders as men of "action and science." Those twin attributes sometimes produced unusual characters like Rock, and unusual situations. Fleeing civil war in 1929, for instance, Rock's entourage crossed the Yangtze River atop inflated goatskins, carrying some of the expedition's yield of more than 20,000 herbarium specimens, seeds of hundreds of plants, 1,703 bird specimens, 900 color Autochrome plates, and 1,800 black-and-white negatives. In addition to hair-raising reading, Rock brought the Western world almost 500 new varieties of rhododendron and blight-resistant chestnut trees. He also introduced GEOGRAPHIC

"A belt of debris perhaps five miles in breadth" challenged Israel C. Russell's group on Alaska's Malaspina Glacier, a union of tributary ice streams covering hundreds of square miles.

readers to the geography and culture of the remote areas he explored.

Pursuing scientific knowledge was by definition a "venture in exploration" during the time of the Society's earliest expeditions. Large chunks of the planet were still practically unknown in 1890, the year NGS President Gardiner Greene Hubbard dispatched geologist and Society founder Israel C. Russell on the first expedition, sponsored jointly with the U.S. Geological Survey.

Russell's orders were formidable: "a geographic reconnoissance [sic] of as large an area as practicable in the St. Elias range, Alaska, including a study of its glacial phenomena, the preparation of a map of the region explored, and the measurement of the height of Mount St. Elias and other neighboring mountains."

On June 28, Russell's party debarked from the frigate *Pinta* in a cold, drenching rain and paddled out of sight into the wilderness of southeastern Alaska. A year later, National Geographic's members read that the work specified in Grant Number 1 had proceeded to the letter. Russell and his topographer recalculated the height and geological positions of Mount St. Elias and several other peaks and sketched hundreds of miles of the area's topography. Russell investigated the formation of glaciers, icebergs, crevasses, and gold-bearing sands.

Russell did something else, equally

Peary aboard the *Roosevelt*, April 1909

ROBERT E. PEARY:
North by Dogsled

Comdr. Robert E. Peary had already made seven expeditions to Greenland and the Arctic when he rose on frostbitten feet to accept the Society's Hubbard Medal for "farthest north" from President Theodore Roosevelt on December 15, 1906. By way of thanks, Peary told the banquet guests that he was far from through: Reaching the North Pole remained "the thing which it is intended that I should do, and the thing that I must do."

He set out on a sweltering July day in 1908, buoyed by cheering New York crowds, siren salutes, and the President's send-off. But his anxiety over the whereabouts of Dr. Frederick A. Cook muted the fanfare. Peary's erstwhile teammate

Struggling through polar pack ice, 1909

had turned archrival when he too set out—more than a year earlier—to stake his name on the Pole.

The expedition ship *Roosevelt*, packed to the gunwales with whale meat, coal, 246 dogs, 49 Eskimos, and 7 Americans, knifed through the ice to Cape Sheridan on Ellesmere Island's northeastern tip. One by one, Peary's military-style relay divisions sledged 90 miles to the Cape Columbia base camp, and from there assaulted the "icy chaos": 413 nautical miles of violent winds, huge pressure ridges, moving floes, and, most treacherous of all, the leads—channels that opened in the ice.

Nevertheless, Peary wired President William Howard Taft from Labrador on September 8, 1909: HAVE HONOR TO PLACE NORTH POLE AT YOUR DISPOSAL. He had lost one team member, young Ross Marvin, drowned in a flaring lead. Taft, however, had already received a nearly identical telegram from Frederick Cook four days earlier.

As controversy raged, lack of proof eroded Cook's claim; so did a reputation already tarnished by past deceptions. Then the suggestion arose that Peary may not have reached the Pole either. As Wally Herbert, a respected Arctic explorer, wrote in NATIONAL GEOGRAPHIC in 1988, neither Peary nor his diary provided essential data, including progressive checks for latitude, longitude, and compass variation. Peary's "astonishingly casual attitude toward the problems of navigation" was compounded by a faulty chronometer and the unpredictable drift of pack ice.

In 1989, a year-long investigation by the Navigation Foundation, commissioned by the Society, analyzed Peary's claims. Using state-of-the-art technology to examine his photographs, it concluded that his camp was probably within five miles of the Pole, about where Peary said it was. Not all critics are convinced. Still, as Herbert wrote, Peary was a pioneer of "exceptional courage" who "extended the bounds of human endeavor."

As determined in repose as at work, Hiram Bingham followed dozens of dead-end leads before making the dizzying climb to find Machu Picchu.

compelling to the GEOGRAPHIC's readers: He brought them along. Writing in a straightforward style, he placed them in the path of avalanches and grizzlies. He could be eloquent about silence and solitude, as when he spent six days alone at the highest camp: "Night came on silently," he wrote, "and with but little change. There was no folding of wings; no twittering of birds in leafy branches; no sighing of winds among rustling leaves.

All was stern and wild and still; there was not a touch of life to relieve the desolation. A midwinter night in inhabited lands was never more solemn. Man had never rested there before."

Usually, brutal slogging precluded reverie. Russell's party struggled around frozen cataracts and up high cliffs from which foaming rivers burst forth. Beyond food, fuel, and tenting, each man was issued only a Hudson Bay blanket, a waterproof coat, a sailor's sou'wester, an alpenstock, a duck sheet, and two lengths of cod-line for an expedition that camped above snow line for 35 days.

One disappointment marred Russell's satisfaction: Storms put St. Elias's summit out of reach. But the discovery of 19,524-foot Mount Logan, Canada's highest peak, helped outweigh the letdown.

Russell's expedition shared much with the five led by botanist Robert F. Griggs between 1915 and 1919. Both men sought the raw challenge of Alaska, a vast wilderness and a natural laboratory that Americans were just beginning to perceive as the back-of-beyond of their own backyard. And both men's expeditions made important discoveries—Griggs's by far the more startling.

In June 1912, ash from an unidentified Alaskan volcano began falling all over the U.S. and Canadian northwest. In Vancouver, acid attacked white linen drying on lines after the Monday washing, and in Port Townsend it corroded the gleaming brass work on automobiles. A brownish volcanic haze drifted to the East Coast.

The source was less than a hundred miles northwest of the Alaskan village of Kodiak, but in a region so remote that even its name—Katmai—was known only to local ships' pilots. Not so after the eruption; it hurled 6.25 cubic miles of ejecta into the atmosphere and ranked among the greatest ever recorded.

Three years later, Robert Griggs and two companions were sent by the Society

"Would anyone believe what I had found?" fretted Hiram Bingham in 1911. Masonry masterwork, the semicircular tower flows into a niched wall of tapering white granite blocks, mortarless and so seamless "they might have grown together." Lofty Huayna Picchu looms to the north.

the absence of secondary activity—fumaroles, mud craters, hot springs—almost always created by huge eruptions, Griggs was at the same time intrigued by the appearance of steamlike clouds in the distance. After several fruitless searches, his group finally found their source—a valley at least 12 miles long, filled with tens of thousands of steam puffs rising from its fissured floor. More than a thousand volcanic vents shot steam columns higher than 500 feet into the air.

"It was," Griggs wrote, "as though all the steam-engines in the world, assembled together, had popped their safety-valves at once and were letting off surplus steam in concert." The Valley of Ten Thousand Smokes named itself.

Griggs lay awake all night, electrified with excitement—and anxiety. Would anyone believe his account of the discovery? He needn't have worried. Soon after

to study revegetation in the volcanic zone. They found pitifully little, except at "green Kodiak"; elsewhere, bleached skeletons of the dead forest poked through the ashes. Sinking into quicksand, swaying atop quaking glaciers of jelled mud, cogwheeling on ash-slick slopes, Griggs also gave up his plan to climb Katmai and peer into its caldera.

Better luck the following year carried Griggs's party to the knife-edged rim "so suddenly that we might almost have walked right over and tumbled down the precipice inside." Some 3,700 feet straight down, a lake the color of robin's eggs nearly filled the two-and-a-half-mile-wide caldera. Ice cliffs and columns of hissing steam ringed it. "Katmai Crater, we thought, was the supreme wonder of the area," Griggs recalled.

A few days later they proved themselves resoundingly wrong. Surprised by

Granite dwellings, below, hewn over generations by workers unfamiliar with iron, stand the test of time. Residents tucked tiny garden plots amid steep terraces linked by more than a hundred stairways that Bingham ranked among the most conspicuous features of Machu Picchu.

the expedition ended, a Washington, D.C., newspaper announced that an "Eighth Wonder of the World" had been found; it was near the "World's Biggest Volcano," headlined another. Griggs's studies of revegetation—an important matter of little popular interest, he noted—had turned into something else altogether.

NATIONAL GEOGRAPHIC's readers were riveted. Would Professor Griggs be returning to the Katmai District in 1917?

If so, one Homer J. Tyla, "well educated, single, 28 years old, extra good health and very strong," wanted to go along. Griggs and several professional colleagues did go back to Alaska the next three years, discovering volcanoes, craters, mountains, lakes, and other features as they studied and mapped the Katmai region.

"Dear Sirs: We are taking great pleasure in Professor Robert Griggs' article," wrote Mary C. Covert from Michigan.

Carved headband and earplugs adorn a 20-ton San Lorenzo basalt, buried for almost 3,000 years. Pouting lips and feline eyes typify a legacy of the Americas' first great sculptors.

Bingham published a book on the subject; Bingham was miffed. The relationship began anew, fitfully, in 1912. NGS agreed to co-sponsor with Yale that year's expedition; then it backed down. Grosvenor explained that "there is considerable feeling that the work is archaeologic and not sufficiently geographic...." Bingham penned a forceful plea, reminding Grosvenor of his avowed interest "in the ruins, the lost cities, and the bones."

Grosvenor finally secured NGS support for the expedition, whose members spent months prying the matted jungle fabric from the ruins and restoring them to an appearance as close as possible to the original. The results were outstanding. Bingham's article, "In the Wonderland of Peru," filled an issue of the GEOGRAPHIC; it included drawings, maps, a foldout panorama, and 234 photographs.

Under renewed Society-Yale sponsorship, Bingham returned in 1914 and 1915 to continue mining Machu Picchu's lode of history. The presence of geologists, topographers, anthropologists, zoologists, botanists, agriculturalists, and osteologists on Bingham's expeditions attested to the widening scope of geographic subjects—which Alexander Graham Bell, the National Geographic's second president, had once expansively defined as "THE WORLD AND ALL THAT IS IN IT."

The $10,000 that Bingham received for his 1912 expedition, the Society's first archaeological grant, set a precedent for a series of discoveries under National Geographic sponsorship. New World archaeology was a particularly fertile field during the Society's first half-century. By the start of World War II, so little work had been done in some areas that an unknown culture could still be unearthed.

One such region was Mexico's Gulf coast. In 1938, Matthew Stirling, an ethnologist and archaeologist with the Smithsonian Institution, endured an eight-hour horseback ride through the humid backwaters of Veracruz to check out stories of a huge basalt head. At Tres Zapotes, he found it buried up to its eyebrows, resembling an upended kettle some 18 feet around. Stirling brushed away enough dirt to photograph his sullen-faced subject. Gracefully carved, it was of a style unlike any then known.

Who had made it? The colossal head reminded Stirling of another mysterious Mexican artifact, a jadeite figurine of a smiling priest, then dated 98 B.C., far earlier than any Maya date known. Could another major civilization have equal share" in financing the expeditions.

Griggs's articles for the GEOGRAPHIC generated the momentum to fulfill his fond hope: In 1918, President Woodrow Wilson proclaimed more than a million acres of Alaska, an area nearly Delaware's size, as Katmai National Monument.

A similar transformation occurred far south in the Peruvian Andes. "Thousands of tourists now visit Machu Picchu," Hiram Bingham wrote several years after he discovered it in 1911. "The traveler can climb the stairways and stroll the plazas where the Inca once paced. And all around, the great silent peaks look down on the secret they guarded so well for three and a half centuries."

Only the faintest clues had led the lanky young professor from Yale there in the first place. In his search, he had investigated every rumor of a ruin when a local Indian gave him one more tantalizing lead. Crawling over rapids on vine-lashed logs, scanning the undergrowth for lethal bushmasters and fer-de-lances, Bingham fought his way, sometimes on all fours, up the mountain called Machu Picchu. The views of green precipices falling thousands of feet to the Urubamba River enchanted Bingham, though a flight of ancient stone terraces didn't impress him as unusual. But the sight beyond a small wood knocked his breath away.

Blanketed in moss and vines and veiled by bamboo thickets were the walls of a whole city of ruined buildings. All were of the finest quality Inca stonework, with granite ashlars fitted so exquisitely that a pin would not penetrate the spaces between them. A cave lined in stone had evidently been a royal mausoleum. It was crowned by a semicircular building—possibly a Temple of the Sun, like

RICHARD H. STEWART

Enigmatic as its Olmec makers, a huge basalt head, one of several that Stirling excavated in Mexico's Veracruz and Tabasco states, emerged at La Venta, 50 miles from a quarry.

Cuzco's—and tied into a long wall. The white granite structures, Bingham wrote later, "surpassed in attractiveness the best Inca walls in Cuzco which had caused visitors to marvel for four centuries."

A steep stairway, one of a hundred, led to a plaza faced by fabulous temples, unique in Bingham's experience, built of 10- and 15-ton blocks. A gabled compound suggested the dwelling place of the ruling Inca himself. Machu Picchu, Bingham realized, was a sanctuary that "had obviously never felt the tramp of a conquistador's boot." It might even be the legendary Vilcabamba, last refuge of the Inca who fled the Spanish in 1537. Bingham's discovery called for thoroughgoing follow-up. Up to then, he had been sponsored solely by Yale University.

Years earlier, Editor Gilbert H. Grosvenor had rebuffed Bingham's proposal for an article on South American archaeology, then courted him the year after

"We have known him ever since he was a little boy and feel sure he would do careful conscientious work." Technology's new tools made his accounts vivid: "With kodaks and halftones and motion pictures to record our discoveries, our advantage over the old-time explorer, who could supplement his account with nothing better than sketches, was enormous."

Griggs repeatedly credited the National Geographic with his triumphs.

Steam jets screen most of the 17-mile-long Valley of 10,000 Smokes from view. Team members cooked over vents and slept on layers of bedding as buffers against the hot ground.

Society President Gilbert H. Grosvenor in turn praised Griggs, his assistants, and—especially—the Society's members, "each of whom, millionaire and college professor, captain of industry and clerk, had an

RAY V. DAVIS

Carlsbad Caverns

Carlsbad Caverns, in southeastern New Mexico, were locally known for their commercial-grade bat guano. But not until 1925, when geologist Willis T. Lee began describing his expedition's findings in NATIONAL GEOGRAPHIC MAGAZINE, did the public become aware of the caverns' stupendous chambers, passageways, and evocative limestone formations.

Giddily, Lee suggested an auto route through the caverns, to be called "To Hades and return by motor." Though his proposal never took shape, Carlsbad Caverns became a national park and one of America's favorite attractions.

RICHARD H. STEWART (BOTH)

Necklace of lead-filled ballast bags, lashed with exploding caps, hangs above Orvil A. Anderson and Albert W. Stevens minutes before *Explorer II* began its ascent to 72,395 feet in 1935.

predated the Maya in southern Mexico?

With photographs in hand and puzzles in mind, Stirling found an enthusiastic co-sponsor in the Society when he returned to Washington. With his wife, Marion, and other expedition members, he set out later the same year, boating inland from the Gulf port of Alvarado through channels choked with purple water hyacinths and canopied by trees full of shrieking parrots.

Matthew and Marion Stirling's professional association with National Geographic spanned more than three decades, and included eight expeditions—co-sponsored by the Smithsonian—to southern Mexico, as well as others to Panama and Ecuador. At Tres Zapotes, the colossal head was speedily excavated. It weighed ten tons, adding to the mystery of its origins: The nearest basalt quarry was ten miles away. Other large basalts, artifacts of a culture without wheels or draft animals, also turned up, along with Maya sculptures.

Stirling's party excavated stelae with delicately carved jaguar faces, solemn jade priests small enough to cup in a hand, and several more huge, helmeted heads from around Veracruz state. Their makers, the Olmec, seemed to have been the Americas' first great artists and lapidaries.

In neighboring Tabasco state, the Olmec town and ceremonial center at La Venta held a great tapering earthen mound, precursor of the Maya pyramids. To the north of it, in a great plaza, two-ton basalt columns enclosed massive burial chambers, each requiring the excavation of tens of thousands of cubic feet of earth. Only a highly developed society with an organized, well-fed labor force could have been capable of such feats.

As intriguing and stubbornly elusive as the Olmec remained, Stirling vividly drew the region's present-day inhabitants in article after article. Among others, he wrote about Damaso, Tres Zapotes' butcher, who appeared regularly in camp to sing ballads for the *americanos*. The cook Nati, a woman with an eight-year-old chaperon, "excelled in making tamales."

Mouth-watering descriptions of meals ran to pages; fiestas punctuated the daily digging; and in an article called "Jungle Housekeeping for a Geographic Expedition," Marion Stirling mentioned "fat juicy worms" dangling and dropping by the dozen from the green thatching of their new jungle abode.

Human continuity, the Stirlings' subtext, had already found a stark counter-

Floodlights and cushioning sawdust ring *Explorer*. Nearly 200 men worked through the night to inflate the ill-fated balloon with 210,000 cubic feet of volatile hydrogen.

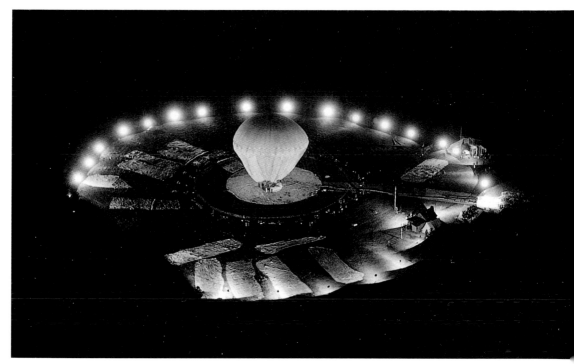

point in distant frontiers, like the stratosphere, where humans had rarely been. Two and a third acres of cotton fabric billowed by hydrogen, *Explorer* was the largest free balloon ever built. In 1934, it lifted three crew members over South Dakota's Badlands to a record 60,613 feet—and then tore. The balloon drifted downward and exploded; the gondola dropped like a stone. After fluttering to safety, *Explorer*'s three crew members gathered up their parachutes, found their wrecked balloon, and vowed to try again.

Two of those three, Albert W. Stevens and Orvil A. Anderson, signaled for *Explorer II*'s ropes to be released on the morning of November 11, 1935. Launched from the same site, the balloon, even larger than its predecessor, soared on helium to 65,000 feet. Tripping sack after

sack of lead ballast, Anderson and Stevens nudged *Explorer II* to 72,395 feet—a record for "farthest aloft" that stood for 21 years.

Very few had ever seen what they did: "From nearly 14 miles above sea level, we saw the earth as a vast expanse of brown...," Stevens wrote. The vision bordered on the apocalyptic: "Sunlight sparkled from rivers and lakes, but we saw no sign of life. It seemed a foreign and lifeless world."

The horizon was a hazy white band; the sky, as they rose, darkened from light blue to bluish black. Stevens and Anderson took photos showing for the first time the boundary between the troposphere and the stratosphere. A ton of scientific instruments clicked and whirred for an hour and a half at the ceiling, gathering information on subjects from cosmic rays

Bottomless balloon, bearing three tons of equipment, becomes a mangled parachute at 7,000 feet. Moments later, it bursts; Commanding Officer Kepner's frantic kick frees Stevens during free-fall as Anderson floats away; Kepner parachutes at 300 feet.

to atmospheric ozone to high-altitude living spores. Then, donning helmets borrowed from Rapid City's high school football team, Anderson and Stevens returned to an eggshell landing a little more than eight hours after they left the earth.

"I thought of a gondola 60,000 feet up in the stratosphere, with pressure of one pound to the square inch," wrote William Beebe. *Explorer*'s ascent, just two weeks earlier that summer of 1934, would have been fresh in his mind. What reminded Beebe of it was his own situation: He had just learned that the bathysphere he was sealed into more than half a mile below the ocean's surface was under pressure of 1,360 pounds to the square inch.

All that kept the pressure in check was a steel cocoon with walls little more than an inch thick. The diving chamber weighed about 5,000 pounds, measured 4 feet 9 inches in diameter, and was lowered and raised on a slender steel cable reeled from the deck of the support ship. A rubber communications hose housed wires for telephone and electric lights. The men carried supplementary oxygen. Beebe himself called the bathysphere "a hollow pea on a swaying cobweb."

Yet under a long, low swell off Bermuda that August day of 1934, naturalist Beebe and marine engineer Otis Barton, who had helped develop the submersible chamber, found themselves dangling at 3,028 feet. They had descended to more than twice the depth of their 1930 record of 1,426 feet, and bested their 1932 record by more than 800 feet. Beebe said later that in offering sponsorship for the 1934 season, Society President Gilbert Grosvenor had demanded "no condition of a new record, which is why I gave it to him." The new record for depth would remain unbroken for 15 years.

Beebe treated NATIONAL GEOGRAPHIC readers to the world of wonder he discovered beneath the surface of the sea.

Impact! Dust billows as *Explorer* crashes into a Nebraska cornfield. Parachutes waft two men to safety; fragments from the explosion, less than a minute earlier, rain down. But barographs survived to mark a ceiling of 60,613 feet, just 624 short of the standing record.

Byrd in hut under Antarctic ice, 1934

Using Bumstead's sun compass, 1947

RICHARD E. BYRD:
South by Airplane

In 1926, Lt. Comdr. Richard E. Byrd, scion of one of Virginia's most prominent families, announced a new era. "The dog sledge must give way to the aircraft," he told a National Geographic audience. He had recently flown over the North Pole, navigating with a sun compass invented by the Society's first chief cartographer, Albert H. Bumstead. Antarctica remained a shimmering frontier that would prompt the Society's extensive support of scientific research and mapping during two separate Byrd Antarctic Expeditions. The first gave Byrd the chance to fulfill his dream of navigating a flight over the South Pole.

On November 28, 1929, his hopes soared on the quivering wings of a stripped-down Ford trimotor, named the *Floyd Bennett* in memory of his beloved former co-pilot. Mechanics checked engines, changed gas lines, and made adjustments. Survival gear—sacks of food, a light sledge, tents, and more—was packed into the fuselage, along with a heavy mapping camera. Byrd and his three companions limited the trimotor's gross weight to 14,500 pounds.

Between Little America, the base camp, and the South Pole, 800 miles away, rose ramparts of high peaks. The plane would have to thread a pass at 10,500 feet, near its absolute ceiling. When air currents turned it into a bobbing cork and the wheel went limp in chief pilot Bernt Balchen's hands, six weeks' worth of emergency rations had to be jettisoned to the ice below.

A forced landing would have meant disaster, but Balchen pulled the plane through the pass and nudged it over the high polar plateau. At the Pole, Byrd dropped an American flag weighted with a stone from Floyd Bennett's grave. Co-pilot Harold June radioed a message to Little America. And from the base's radio towers, news of the polar conquest was broadcast to a marveling world. Byrd and his crew circled the Pole twice and returned to base—a 1,500-mile round-trip made in less than 19 hours.

"Admiral of the Ends of the Earth," Richard Evelyn Byrd had met a more skeptical reaction by predicting that regular flights over the Poles would be made by the 1950s. But it was a forecast borne out in his lifetime.

An area in Antarctica where glaciers meet, photographed during a 1947 mission

The Ford trimotor *Floyd Bennett* that carried Byrd to the South Pole in 1929

ELSE BOSTELMANN

In one of many paintings created in the early 1930s on the basis of naturalist William Beebe's descriptions, the flashing fangs of a saber-toothed viperfish doom tiny ocean sunfish despite their spiny armor. One of the seven-inch carnivores even charged Beebe's bathysphere at 1,700 feet.

Houdini-like, Beebe wriggles through the bathysphere's 14-inch opening after a 1934 dive. Steam-driven winches ran the *Ready*'s boom, shown supporting the 5,000-pound chamber.

Nose pressed against a cold quartz window, he saw huge schools of fish, their lights twinkling in the darkness like a metropolis seen from an airliner at night. Explosions of flame seemed to burst in his face as great deep-sea shrimps loosed their defenses against the bathysphere.

Beebe described wholly unknown fish. At 1,900 feet, one he called the Five-lined Constellationfish appeared, outlined in curving bands of yellow and purple lights. Less fetching was the two-foot Pallid Sailfin, "the hue of water-soaked flesh, an unhealthy buff."

Many other scientists thought Beebe a showman and his rhapsodies of the deep little more than fish stories. One perceived Beebe's assigning generic and species names to creatures "faintly seen through the bathysphere windows" as an outrageous breach of scientific procedure. Perhaps the last word belonged to Rachel Carson, though. In her visionary book *The Sea Around Us*, she credited William Beebe

with stimulating her absorption in "the mystery and meaning of the sea." And so it was for thousands of others.

To a jaded colleague Beebe once snapped that boredom was "immoral"; to the public he conveyed his belief that "the most thrilling adventure stories" were nature's own. Beebe was humbled by nature, and not overly impressed with the man-made contraptions that seemed to tame its forces. And, more than most, he could sense his kinship with other scientific explorers, whether stratospheric balloonists or space travelers of the future, hurtling through a black place where "the shining planets, comets, suns, and stars must be closely akin to the world of life as it appears to the eyes of an awed human being, in the open ocean, one half mile down."

A half century and more after Beebe's record dives, the ocean depths still remain a terra incognita, their myriad life forms uncounted, their impact on global ecology

Each step punctuated by gasps for air, Everest-bound climbers struggle up Lhotse toward Camp V, 26,200 feet up the South Col. Limestone tints the Yellow Band, a well-known landmark.

Seated in deference to 70-mph gusts, Barry Bishop clutches American and NGS flags at the summit. First, though, he and Lute Jerstad crumpled and wept with joy and relief.

BARRY C. BISHOP/NATIONAL GEOGRAPHIC STAFF (PRECEDING PAGES); LUTHER G. JERSTAD

ill understood, their spectacular canyons and mountains murkily outlined. Even the world's craggy roofs have yielded far more easily—which is to say, with awesome difficulty. But as the nature of scientific exploration itself changes, electronic eyes have begun to scan the depths, and sophisticated remotely operated vehicles (ROVs) are capable of probing the farthest corners.

As Barry C. Bishop, vice president for Research and Exploration, explains, "At the time the traditional terrae incognitae were being filled in, science was becoming more and more sophisticated. Now technology allows us to explore unknown territories—the deep sea, the planet from space, secrets of biodiversity."

On the three-tenths of the planet not shrouded by water, a final frontier closed with the ascent of Mount Everest. The 29,028-foot mountain had repelled seven major expeditions before Edmund Hillary and Tenzing Norgay reached its summit in 1953. Ten years later, the Society along with many other research organizations sponsored the first American Mount Everest Expedition, during which six team members reached the summit via two separate routes.

Barry Bishop defines the 1963 expedition as one that marked the end and beginning of eras. As a team member, he should know. "It was one of the last of the true, classic, 'golden age' expeditions in terms of mountaineering and exploration and teamwork," he recalls. "But we also used the mountain as the highest scientific field laboratory on the planet, carrying out five different research programs. One involved the use of low molecular tritium to measure the effects of high altitude on the adrenal cortex. The psychological work was an outgrowth of World War II studies on how stress affects personality."

Three decades later, what remains most vivid and memorable about the expedition to him may sound surprising. "It's not reliving how Lute Jerstad and I attained the summit," he says readily. Nor is it the nightmarish, nauseous fatigue from oxygen deprivation, nor spending a night at 28,000 feet without a tent or sleeping bag. Nor that night's legacy: the loss of toes and finger parts to gangrene.

Instead, he singles out the human factor. "Teamwork. Every member was selected on the basis of his ability to lead when required and follow when required. We went out as friends, and despite our disagreements, came back even closer friends. That was the ultimate experience." He notes sadly that the focus today seems to be more on improved equipment and technology.

On May 22, 1963, Bishop and Jerstad roped themselves together and began their descent from the summit, leaving American and NGS flags whipping in the wind. Suddenly, Bishop saw the rope between them catch on a cornice edge and draw him inexorably toward its precipice. Shouting ahead to Jerstad in the 70-mile gust was futile. "He was totally unaware, and starting to lose his vision because the wind was blowing snow crystals into his goggles. If I'd gone over, I would have been unconscious within 30 seconds, but Lute wouldn't have cut the rope, and he too might have died of hypothermia."

Instead, in less time than it takes to read these words, Bishop freed himself of the rope, let it whip from the cornice, and

THOMAS J. ABERCROMBIE/NATIONAL GEOGRAPHIC STAFF

Severely frostbitten, a bareheaded Bishop awaits evacuation with William Unsoeld, who helped pioneer the West Ridge summit route.

then reattached it to his waist. "Fear sometimes comes only in retrospect," he says. "In an emergency, the oxygen-starved mind has no room for fear."

From an office at Society headquarters in Washington, D.C., Bishop reviews applications for Grant Number 5,000 for field research. As the nature of exploration changes, he and his colleagues continue to look for scientific merit and geographical scope—and still, in the uniqueness of enterprises followed for their own sake, for the hint of adventure.

The Search for
Human Beginnings

"**A**lways something new out of Africa" wrote Pliny the Elder, the Roman scholar, 2,000 years ago. "And always the oldest," Louis Leakey might have added. On his first visit to the Society in 1959, the Kenya-born

GORDON GAHAN (PRECEDING PAGES); MRS. L. J. BEECHER

On leave from Cambridge in 1924, Louis Leakey pauses during his first East African dig, for dinosaurs.

Preceding Pages: Dawn at Koobi Fora finds Richard Leakey, seated, and colleagues sorting fossils. The 1969 trove included two hominid skulls.

anthropologist reached into the cotton-wool wrappings inside a padded case, rustled around, and with a showman's flair, retrieved a discovery sure to impress the Committee for Research and Exploration: a remarkably complete skull that

Leakey believed was 600,000 years old and belonged to the earliest known human ancestor.

The discovery was a fitting event for the hundredth anniversary of Charles Darwin's *On the Origin of Species*. In 1859, the book had stunned Victorian society. The first printing sold out in a day, an eminent scientist pronounced evolution "the law of higgeldy-piggeldy," and clerics professed moral outrage—even though only one sentence in the book implicated humans in the theory of evolution. "Light will be thrown," Darwin predicted, "on the origin of man and his history."

With his controversial announcement, Leakey shed as much heat as light on humanity's distant past. Leading contenders for the title of "oldest man," such as Peking Man and Java Man, were *Homo erectus*, the much more recent species that preceded our own *Homo sapiens*. Sweeping them aside, Leakey honored Darwin's belief that Africa would prove to be the human cradle.

Leakey named the skull *Zinjanthropus boisei*, East African Man. (The species name honored a benefactor, Charles Boise.) Scientists coined "Zinj." Between themselves, Leakey and his wife, Mary, an archaeologist who actually discovered it, called the fossil "Dear Boy." And with good reason. It made Leakey a household name, ensured support from the Society, and justified the Leakeys' decades-long search for hominid fossils in Tanzania's Olduvai Gorge.

Scientists rate the chances of a hominid fossil like Zinj surviving for hundreds of thousands of years as infinitesimal. Still, when Leakey first began prospecting there in 1931, Olduvai struck the tall, dark missionary's son as

particularly promising. As one of several ancient lakes along Africa's Great Rift Valley, it would have drawn many creatures. Much later, a river sliced through the sediments that covered the dry lake bed, creating the gorge. A scramble from sisal-covered rim to dusty floor, 300 feet down, takes only minutes—or two million years, hurtling past strata to bedrock.

It was there, by the old lakeshore, that the Leakeys began finding stone tools. Louis had collected ancient tools from all over East Africa, but Olduvai's crudely flaked cobbles were much more primitive. Somewhere, he believed, there had to be the remains of an extremely prim-

Louis Leakey displays some of his fossil finds at Tanzania's Olduvai Gorge: a palm-filling *Deinotherium* molar and an extinct elephant's tooth.

itive toolmaker. Trekking down from their Nairobi home and turning around when food ran out, Louis and Mary spent season after field season searching for him.

Finally, one July morning in 1959, the search paid off. Zinj, reassembled from hundreds of pieces, was the unmistakable portrait of a hominid, a primate that, like modern humans, negotiated his world on two legs. But what sort of a hominid? Kin to the small-brained, big-faced, apelike

DES BARTLETT/ARMAND DENIS PRODUCTIONS; GILBERT M. GROSVENOR/NATIONAL GEOGRAPHIC STAFF (RIGHT)

australopithecines, *A. africanus* and *A. robustus,* whose fossils had been found in South Africa? Or was he *Homo,* the toolmaker with the enlarged brain and smaller, more delicately turned features?

"People will say he is NOT human but he is," Louis penned in his field journal. Though Zinj's huge dished face and bony head crest looked even less human than the australopithecines', he was, after all, found amid stone tools. And toolmaking, Louis believed, was humanity's hallmark.

Zinj was no man, but as it turned out, he lived much, much earlier than even Leakey had supposed. Coincidentally, the anniversary of *On the Origin of Species* also brought forth a revolutionary method of chemically dating volcanic deposits such as Olduvai's and, indirectly, fossils within them. Potassium-argon dating used sensitive instruments to measure the rate of decay of radioactive potassium into argon gas. The volcanic tuff that yielded Zinj was repeatedly tested: 1.8 million years, came the result, making Zinj the first reliably dated hominid.

Even so, Leakey himself almost immediately deposed Zinj the Earliest Man. In 1960, more hominid remains surfaced at Olduvai. They were about the same age as Zinj, but there the similarities faded. Though poorly preserved, the skulls had clearly encased bigger brains—big enough, argued Leakey, to cross the "cerebral Rubicon" dividing apes from humans. The jaws anchored smaller cheek teeth than Zinj's massive nutcrackers. Fine-boned hands were capable of a

GORDON GAHAN

Father and son ponder a fossil monkey skull at Koobi Fora, Richard Leakey's 1969 camp in northern Kenya. His first solo venture, on Lake Turkana's western shore, yielded hominid skulls.

The family tree seemed to be sprouting new limbs. And at the same time the Leakey family itself was branching in different directions.

precision grip. Here was the *real* toolmaker of Olduvai, Leakey insisted, demoting Zinj to australopithecine status. Here, he announced, was *Homo habilis,* or handy man, the earliest known human.

Leakey had just tripled *Homo*'s known age. He also dropped a new player onto the stage shared 1.8 million years ago by two australopithecines, Olduvai's *A. boisei,* Zinj, and South Africa's similar *A. robustus; A. africanus* had preceded them.

Louis shed his khaki coveralls and suited up for the constant round of lectures, fund raising, and black-tie events that filled his last years. Mary, though, dug in at Olduvai. With her passion for stone tools, she recorded the exact location and details of more than 37,000 choppers, hand axes, cleavers, cobbles, and other tools from Olduvai's oldest beds. Her work changed archaeology

Close-up work consumes Richard Leakey and Kamoya Kimeu at West Turkana. Kimeu's initial find, a skull fragment, led to discovering most of a 1.6-million-year-old skeleton.

and inspired much of what is now known about how the earliest humans lived.

But increasingly, it was Richard Leakey, the second of Mary and Louis's three sons, who claimed the spotlight. As a lanky teenager nicknamed Ostrich, he had shared his mother's aversion to formal education, dropping out of school to start a safari business. But when he returned to the fossil-hunting fold, Richard couldn't wait to sidestep Louis's long shadow. In 1968, he unexpectedly asked the Society to support work at an entirely new and unproven site by Lake Turkana in northern Kenya. Though the elder Leakey argued against the idea, Richard received his grant.

He had spied his site by chance when the six-seater flying him to Omo from Nairobi detoured around a thunderhead. Helicoptering into the desolate area a few days later, he confirmed his hunch that it was an ancient lake bed, a geological jumble grooved by sandstone gullies, swirled with ash, and strewn with fossils. Koobi Fora, the camp Leakey set up, was named for a slender sandspit. By day, a yellowish shimmer rises off the sizzling moonscape surrounding it. By night, crocodile eyes glitter red in the water.

There, in 1969, a decade after Zinj was found, two hominid skulls turned up and proved to be *Australopithecus boisei*, like Zinj. At age 24, Richard Leakey had

Rift Valley Geology

Hot springs hiss skyward at Kenya's Lake Bogoria as Africa continues to rupture—as it has for millions of years—along a crack in the earth's crust called the Great Rift Valley. The rift extends from southeastern Africa to southwestern Asia. The Red Sea fills one branch of the Y-shaped rift, and the Gulf of Aden fills the other. In Africa, a series of

DAVID L. BRILL

parallel geologic faults cuts
through the crust. Over the years,
land outside the faults moved farther apart while land between them
dropped, forming a valley whose
walls reveal fossil-rich strata.

Olduvai Gorge, Lake Turkana,
Laetoli: All of East Africa's major
hominid sites lie in the Rift Valley;
Ethiopia's complex Afar Triangle
marks the place where the rift
branches into its Y shape.

Frozen in time and cementlike ash, a 3.6-million-year-old footprint offers Mary Leakey a measure of humanity's past at Laetoli. Most scientists link our beginnings to an upright gait.

equaled a discovery his parents had made after a three-decade search.

Then he outdid them. Actually, Bernard Ngeneo found the first fragments of the famous Skull 1470, and Richard's wife, Meave, a zoologist, painstakingly reassembled about 150 of them. But nobody was more delighted than Richard with the result: a thin, high, rounded skull with a cranial capacity that clearly put it in the *Homo* camp. Known by its accession number, KNM-ER 1470 was in much better condition than Olduvai's *Homo habilis.*

Its brain was much larger, and at first it appeared to be much older, nearly three million years old.

"Either we toss out this skull or we toss out our theories of early man," Richard Leakey told the GEOGRAPHIC's readers. The "theories" that he would dismiss argued that *Homo*, including modern humans, evolved from the more ape-like australopithecines. The Leakeys, particularly Louis, believed that the human evolutionary line was very old, very pure, and very independent of the australopithecines. If 1470, a *Homo habilis*, lived *before* the australopithecines, then he couldn't have been their descendant.

Richard had eased the skull into his Cessna and flown it down to Nairobi. Louis, ailing, turned the fragile skull in his

hands and marveled. A few days later, in London on the first leg of a lecture tour, Louis had a massive heart attack and died later that Sunday morning.

But many scientists were suspicious of the claim that such an advanced-looking being had lived so long ago; animal fossils found near it also looked relatively modern. Years later, Richard Leakey finally agreed: Undeniable new evidence proved 1470 about 1.9 million years old—roughly Zinj's age. But the two skulls share more than a date. Each is one of the most important hominid fossils ever found, each was at first mistakenly dated, and each made a Leakey famous.

That fame galvanized a generation of scientists. Donald Johanson, for one, was still in school when he read about Zinj in

Who left the trails in the ash of the volcano? One hominid stood 4'8"; another, just 4'; an artist imagined a family group, but no one knows.

a 1960 GEOGRAPHIC. "The name Olduvai," he recalls, "with its hollow, exotic sound, rang in my head like a struck gong." Born to a cleaning lady and a barber, both Swedish immigrants, the Chicago teen decided that he too "could make a career out of digging up fossils." He was about the same age as Richard Leakey.

By 1973, Johanson had an assistant professorship in anthropology. Richard Leakey had 1470. He also had Johanson's admiration for his boldness in staking his reputation on a relatively unproven area, East Turkana.

Shell of humanity, the curving skull of KNM-ER 1470 encased a brain belonging to *Homo habilis*, the first large-brained hominid species known. An artist added teeth and jaw, shaded brown, less massive than *Australopithecus*'s.

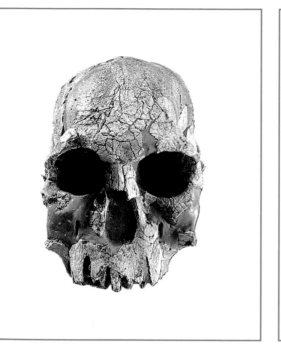

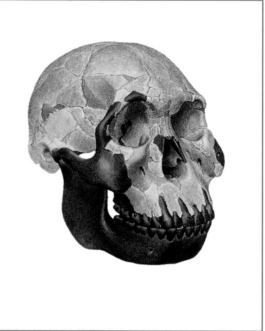

Johanson was about to embark on a similar venture. His site, like Leakey's, was an ancient lake bed drowned in sediments. It lay in Ethiopia's Afar Desert, a chink in the earth's crust that links Africa's Rift Valley to rift systems under the Red Sea and the Gulf of Aden. Tilted and broken by faulting, the Afar is gouged by rivers that boil over during seasonal flooding and uncover fossils. Johanson's team began prospecting in the badlands where the Hadar River cuts a 50-foot gorge through a layer cake of time. Three million years of time, at least.

One 110-degree day in 1974, Johanson noticed an arm bone poking out of a gully's slope. It might have been a monkey's—but, no, it lacked the monkey's bony flange. Johanson felt his pulse racing. He and graduate student Tom Gray looked around: Pieces of skull, thighbone, vertebrae, female pelvis, ribs, and other bones littered the ground. It looked like the skeleton of a single individual. The two scientists, sweaty and smelly as two hominids ever were, hugged, danced, howled, jumped up and down, and tore back to camp with their Land-Rover's horn blaring.

"That first night we never went to bed at all," Johanson recalled. Their tape recorder blasted the Beatles' "Lucy in the Sky with Diamonds" into the night, over and over. They named their skeleton Lucy, though the Ethiopians called her Denkenesh: "You are wonderful." Either way, she was more precious than diamonds. Three-million-year-old Lucy was the oldest and indeed the first collection of hominid bones complete enough to be called a skeleton.

She was startlingly different too, a

Next: eyes, ears, fat, cartilage, and muscles; the nose remains apelike. Finally, "1470 Man," or Woman—based on one interpretation of the relatively delicate, 1.9-million-year-old skull, about half the size of a modern human's.

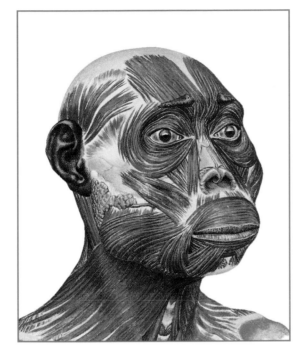 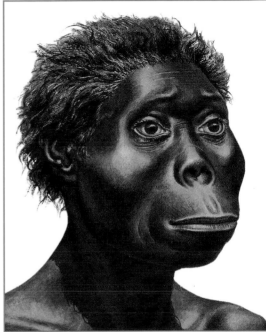

primitive little adult some three-and-a-half feet tall, with a tiny skull—about softball size, Johanson guessed—completely erupted wisdom teeth, upright gait, and the beginnings of arthritis.

The following season, with NGS support, a cascade of new hominid finds simultaneously brightened and muddied the picture. It began with teeth and bits of bone emerging from the dust at Hadar. They pointed the way to nearly 200 other hominid fossils from Site 333—jaws, teeth, leg bones, even part of a baby's skull. All told, the remains of 13 individuals were found, including young and old adults and children. The adults varied dramatically in size.

They became known as the First Fam-ily—perhaps not a family at all but a cohesive group of some kind, hinting at the origins of humanness in cooperative behavior. As they had lived together, so the First Family died close together, perhaps trapped by a flash flood.

Hints of humanness also struck Mary Leakey in 1978, when parallel trails of fossil hominid footprints were exposed at Laetoli, a thickety, snake-infested site near Olduvai. About 3.6 million years ago, three hominids walked north through a layer of wet ash deposited by a nearby volcano. Like a new concrete sidewalk, the ash held the impressions as it dried into trona, a mineral formation.

Before vegetation concealed them again, the footprints offered proof that those hominids walked upright on feet whose form is the same as modern humans'. One stood about four feet

eight inches; another stood just four feet.

The smaller one, Mary Leakey noticed, stopped, paused, and turned at one point. "This motion, so intensely human, transcends time," she wrote. "Three million six hundred thousand years ago, a remote ancestor—just as you or I—experienced a moment of doubt."

Whoever these hominids were, their kind had much in common with the Hadar hominids. After studying all the known characteristics of hominid fossils from both Hadar and Laetoli, Johanson and a colleague, Tim White, in 1978 named a new species, *Australopithecus*

afarensis, that included all of the Hadar and Laetoli fossils. *A. afarensis*, they claimed, was the long-sought common ancestor of both *Homo* and the younger australopithecines.

The announcement fell like an ax between the Leakeys and Johanson. Mary believed that all the Laetoli fossils and the larger ones from Hadar were *Homo*. Richard insisted that two distinct species, one *Homo* and the other *Australopithecus*, had coexisted in both places. The quest continued for *Homo*'s ancestors.

"Rival Anthropologists Divide on 'Pre-Human' Find" ran one headline at

Badlands by Ethiopia's Awash River yield Donald Johanson a Pliocene horse mandible. At another site, designated 333 (above), his dental pick pries at matrix encasing part of a distinctly *Homo* femur.

the time *A. afarensis* was introduced to the world. Since then, most paleoanthropologists—though not Richard Leakey— have swung round to Johanson's and White's viewpoint. But as Johanson himself says, few in his field would bet on the look of any family tree. "Virtually everyone would place *A. afarensis* at the stem. But what happens next is harder to know because fossils between two and three million years old are really rare."

So when the mysterious "Black Skull" emerged from the middle of that period, some scientists again pruned and grafted their evolutionary trees. Alan Walker, a paleontologist working with Richard Leakey on an NGS project near Lake Turkana's west shore, found the 2.5-million-year-old skull in 1985. Well preserved, it seemed to share characteristics of both Lucy's kind, *A. afarensis,* and *A. boisei,* stretching *A. boisei*'s lineage back and suggesting a transitional creature.

The very next season, "Turkana Boy" emerged from the human hothouse of West Turkana. The skull and skeleton that Kamoya Kimeu, Leakey's longtime colleague, found were about 1.6 million years old—the oldest known example of *Homo erectus.* Turkana Boy lived to be

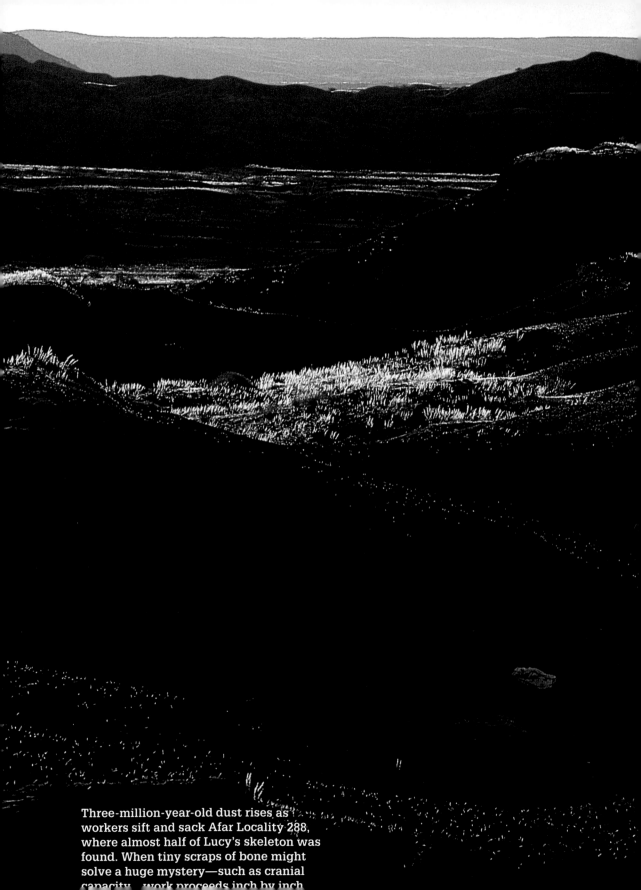

Three-million-year-old dust rises as
workers sift and sack Afar Locality 288,
where almost half of Lucy's skeleton was
found. When tiny scraps of bone might
solve a huge mystery—such as cranial
capacity—work proceeds inch by inch.

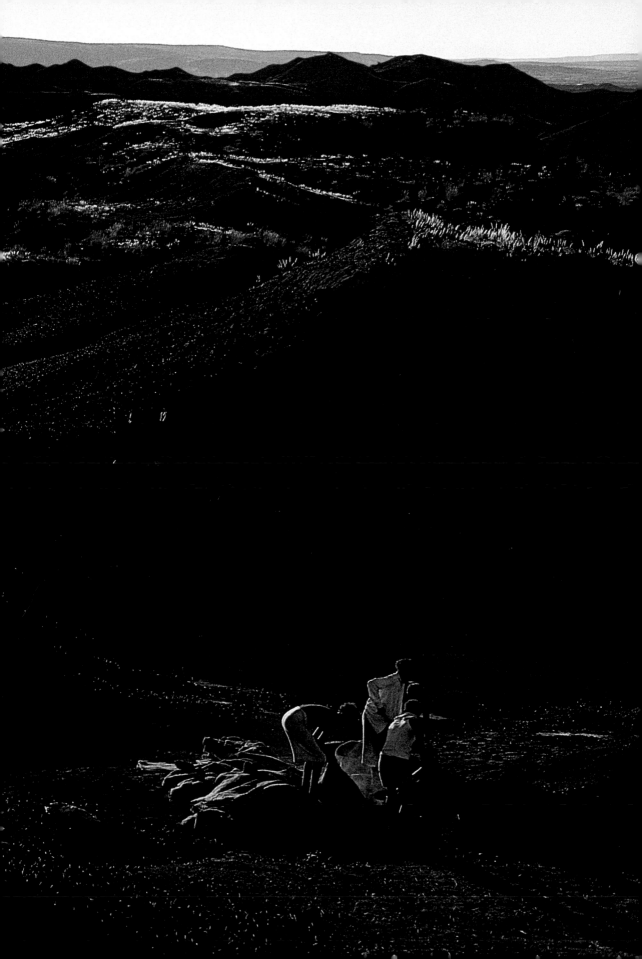

about 11 and, surprisingly, grew to 5'4", taller than most modern boys his age.

But exciting new fossil finds are rare. The bones business, by its nature, proceeds jerkily, through fits of discovery, false starts, fallow periods. Careers wind down or, like Richard Leakey's—which turned to the plight of African wildlife— are diverted. There are maddening interruptions: Political conditions kept Don Johanson and many of his colleagues out of Ethiopia for nearly 15 years. There are constant challenges to stated theory: No sooner was Johanson's team back in the Afar in 1990 than a large upper jaw was found; it was Lucy's age but different enough that some scientists declared that a second hominid had coexisted with her kind.

Traditionally, words like "first," "ear-

DAVID L. BRILL

ALAN WALKER

Alan Walker (left) and Richard Leakey study the cranium of "Turkana Boy." A cast of Walker's "Black Skull" (above) shows the bony crest, huge jaw, and small braincase that sparked new questions about evolutionary change.

liest," and "oldest" have burnished fossils and their finders. In 1992, though, Johanson's team was elated to find newer fossil-bearing deposits and hominid fossils that extend Hadar's horizon to the brink of the fossil "black hole," between two and three million years ago. As Johanson explains, "Our missing link is the bridge between *A. afarensis* and the larger-brained *Homo*. It looks like *Homo* emerged during that million-year period." Stone tools, 2.5 million years old, have already been found in the Hadar area.

"Those million years were a very important time for hominids everywhere," Johanson says. From related studies comes evidence of catastrophic climate change about 2.5 million years ago. In Ethiopia, moist woodland abruptly gave way to dry savanna. Did the change and the challenge create *Homo*? Perhaps not. But even so, Johanson says, "The question of questions is: What is our relationship with the natural world? If we can run the clock back to Lucy's time and start the tape over again, it might indeed reawaken our awareness that we are part of the natural web and our respect for the world around us."

Peoples Past and Present

By Ron Fisher

From the shadows of the past they seem to cry out to us, as if determined to explain themselves. This is how we lived, they seem to say; this is what we believed; these were our possessions; these our families; these our joys and our terrors.

Today we study the fragments of the lives they left behind. Anthropologists probe their origins and societies and relationships, using as tools a number of subdisciplines—including archaeology, which looks at the physical evidence of previous cultures, whether fossils, artifacts, or monuments.

"Peering into the face of a skeleton...an archaeologist cannot help but be aware that he is eyeball to eyesocket with someone who knew the answers to many, if not all, the questions he is asking," wrote archaeologist Ivor Noël Hume. "Our hands touch, but the silence of eternity holds us apart."

Since its founding in 1888, the Society has sponsored nearly 700 research projects in the broad field of anthropology, which includes—in addition to archaeology—physical anthropology, ethnology, and paleoanthropology. Hundreds of grants have supported archaeology, the sifting and sorting of the detritus left by peoples in every era and in every corner of the globe, from Voidokoilia in Greece to the Aleutian Islands and from the frozen

Images from humanity's distant past evoke wonder. Who drew them? Why? Anthropologists study such sites as France's Lascaux cave for clues.

Preceding Pages: Straining workmen rebuild 2,000-year-old Aphrodisias in Turkey—one of many archaeological projects supported by the Society.

images contradicts our notion of the brutish "caveman." The art itself raises questions that archaeologists ponder: Is that a spear in the flank of that bison or merely a bush? If a spear, does it mean the painter first "killed" the animal on the cave wall in order to ensure success later during the actual hunt? Or is it just the accidental overlapping of images? Is that the sun rising in the background? Does it have an astronomical significance? Or is the whole scene just doodling?

French prehistorian and archaeologist Jean-Philippe Rigaud remembers visiting the cave at Lascaux with his parents many years ago. The spooky paintings evoked for him images of "an icy and hostile world" that continued to intrigue him into adulthood. National Geographic research grants he received in 1987 and in 1988 supported his investigation of "Grotte XVI" near Castelnaud, in France. Working with the larger field crew made possible by the grants, Dr. Rigaud found artifacts—beads and buttons, antler projectile points, and harpoons—that dated back to the Late Pleistocene epoch.

In a related field, grants to Alexander Marshack, research associate at Harvard's Peabody Museum, have helped him develop analytic techniques—such as microscopy, and infrared and ultraviolet photography—for studying prehistoric symbol systems, the nonverbal ways early humans communicated with one another. Pre-arithmetic Upper Paleolithic notations, Ice Age cave paintings, prehistoric incised slates from the American Southwest, and various Central American artifacts he has studied have all contributed to our knowledge of early man.

Traditionally, archaeology has been a terrestrial discipline, but that began changing in the early 1960s. Since 1961, research grants have contributed

SISSE BRIMBERG

Bas-relief bison emerges from a 16,000-year-old limestone slab in a shelter near Lascaux. Unknowingly, Paleolithic artists documented their world for today's anthropologists.

tips of the Andes to the dark Mediterranean depths. In the fields of ethnology, physical anthropology, and paleoanthropology, many grants have focused on the differing aspects of human culture— from the magic and religion of Suriname to the depopulation of the islands of western Ireland and the role of women in the Pokot tribe of Kenya.

Archaeology begins in the cool, dark depths of caves, where ancient people painted their world on the walls and ceilings. The confident beauty of the significantly to the efforts of George Bass of Texas A&M University to help develop a new field—underwater archaeology. Treasure hunters and salvagers had long been active beneath the seas, recovering much valuable and interesting material but destroying precious archaeological sites in the process.

Dr. Bass's first encounter with a sunken ship was in 1960, when he dived on a Bronze Age wreck off the coast of Turkey, an expedition supported largely by the University Museum of the University of Pennsylvania. Bass learned to dive so that he could supervise excavations himself. The first night they anchored over the dive site, he later wrote, "I knew it was the beginning of an adventure. I did not know that it was the beginning of a way of life."

Bass was determined to bring to underwater archaeology the same scientific rigor and discipline that topside scientists brought to surface archaeology. He insisted on careful excavation and meticulous record keeping, and on archaeologists diving, rather than leaving the underwater work to others. He believed that sites underwater should be surveyed and excavated stratigraphically—layer by layer—just as digs were on land. He accurately recorded sites and uncovered objects by measurement, drawing, and photography, and then published detailed reports.

In 1961, the Society began supporting Bass's work. His first article in NATIONAL GEOGRAPHIC—"Underwater Archeology: Key to History's Warehouse"—was published in 1963 and chronicled his work on a Byzantine ship wrecked off Turkey 13 centuries ago. The wreck lay 120 feet deep, and divers spent only 43 minutes a day working on it in order to avoid the deadly bends. Pipe scaffolding—built in nine descending steps to accommodate the slope of the seafloor—covered the

ALEXANDER MARSHACK

"Fat, abundant...female in a crown of matronly waves," grantee Alexander Marshack calls the 26,000-year-old Willendorf Venus, found in Austria.

wreck, and two 13-foot towers held cameras in a fixed focus. "Thus we could take grid photographs quickly at each step of the scaffolding," Bass wrote. "We could plot planks and nail holes exactly to the centimeter. The time-consuming business of drawing underwater was practically eliminated, and underwater archeology had moved another stride forward." An air-filled, plastic-coated cloth balloon lifted heavy artifacts to the surface, and an airlift acted as a vacuum cleaner, hoisting small, lightweight objects to a collecting bag, which held

Laying a grid, marine archaeologists mimic topside colleagues with painstaking techniques. Grantee George Bass developed such methods, here being used on a wreck off Turkey.

them until they could be sifted and examined topside.

The wreck helped historians understand the link between the older ships of the Romans and the more modern wooden craft of the Mediterranean. The ship's planks above the waterline were not edge-joined as in earlier Roman ships, but nailed to frames and probably caulked. "We had found the transition to modern ship construction," Bass said.

Bass felt he had even made a human contact with the past. An inscription emerged, punched into a bronze bar: "George, Senior Sea Captain," it said, in Greek. "And so, from the mists of the

BILL CURTSINGER

wreck from the 14th century B.C. off Ulu Burun, Turkey, marine archaeology had become more sophisticated. Now Bass could interpret his findings in a way that shed new light on the patterns of trade and commerce in the late Bronze Age.

The ship lay on a steep slope, 140 to 170 feet underwater—divers could spend only 20 minutes twice a day working on it—and carried as its principal cargo about 350 copper ingots. The contents of what Bass called his "cargo vessel" apparently came from at least seven cultures: Mycenaean Greek, Canaanite, Cypriot, Egyptian, Kassite, Assyrian, and Nubian. There were copper from Cyprus; daggers, an amphora full of glass beads, and cobalt-blue glass disks, probably from Canaan; ivory from Syria or Africa; amber beads from the Baltic; scarabs of bone and ivory—a gold one bearing the name of Nefertiti—from Egypt; *Pistacia* resin for making incense from the eastern Mediterranean.

Clearly, by the time the ship sank, a well-established network existed for trading among the various ethnic and linguistic groups around the Mediterranean. The ships evidently sailed from Syria-Palestine to Cyprus, to the Aegean and occasionally Sardinia, then back by way of North Africa.

Another vessel—from an era 1,500 years later but only 750 miles away—was examined by J. Richard Steffy, a Society grant recipient from the Institute of Nautical Archaeology, founded by Dr. Bass, at Texas A&M University.

High and dry, the boat was discovered buried upside down in Herculaneum, a Roman fishing port of 4,000 people that was destroyed, like its neighbor Pompeii, by an eruption of Mount

centuries, emerged a man," wrote Bass.

For more than 30 years, Bass has received financial support from the Society. Most of his work has been conducted in the Mediterranean. As he wrote, "Virtually everything made by man, from tiny obsidian blades to huge temple columns, was carried at one time or another in a ship, and much was lost at sea."

By 1984, when he began work on a

George Bass (in light-blue shirt) lunches with his crew of mostly Turkish scholars and students. They worked this site, a thousand-year-old wreck rich in medieval glass, in 1978.

Vesuvius in A.D. 79. The black clouds of ash and gas that swept across the city in August obliterated it and most of its inhabitants. Many of them were craftsmen and artisans. The city was also home to a core of affluent and cultured people. Author Joseph Deiss called Herculaneum "a time capsule for posterity."

The vessel that interested Dr. Steffy was about 30 feet long and had been carbonized by the heat of the eruption; it was otherwise undamaged. "Many of the ships and boats uncovered by archaeologists were victims of violent events," wrote Steffy, "but few, if any, were wrecked more dramatically than the Herculaneum boat." It lay face down, its inverted hull covering and preserving its interior. Steffy observed, "This will be *the* definitive Roman boat," a class of vessel about which little was known. He found the Romans' work-

manship "on a par with the Greeks', and their shipbuilders were as meticulous as cabinetmakers."

"The Herculaneum boat was built by a well disciplined boatwright," noted Steffy. "There is a lot of good joinery work...and construction as a whole indicates plenty of pride and expertise."

"The most important question concerns the boat's purpose," he wrote. "Certainly it was not a coastal cargo vessel or lighter; it seems too shallow and lightly built for that. Undoubtedly it was intended to be primarily a rowed vessel; the suggested open area, low freeboard, relatively narrow beam, and what appears to be poor lateral resistance for sailing all point to oars as the primary means of propulsion....I suspect one of two functions for this vessel—that of a tugboat or of a fishing vessel used in seining operations."

The Society's research committee first became involved at Herculaneum because of an urgent appeal. In 1980, archaeologists were excavating some ancient structures at the site when a drainage system failed. Workmen began digging a trench to divert the water from the site. A skeleton emerged; then another, and another, all beautifully preserved. They had been buried there for 1,900 years. But as sunlight and air reached them, they began to deteriorate.

Officials in Herculaneum appealed to the world for help in studying and protecting the skeletons before they were lost forever. The Society immediately funded Sara Bisel, a physical anthropologist and archaeologist, to hurry to Herculaneum. "Who says dead men don't talk," she said as she began work. She first washed the bones with a soft toothbrush, then allowed them to dry for a few days. Dipped in an acrylic-plastic emulsion and dried, the bones were ready for reconstruction.

After 150 skeletons had been found,

Bisel called the site "a very major find, the first Roman population we ever had to study. It's the first time we've known what ancient Romans really looked like." A few skeletons had been found at Pompeii, but they had disintegrated before they could be studied.

Bisel found that, except for the slaves, the people of Herculaneum generally were in good health. The men averaged 5 feet 7 inches tall, the women 5 feet 1½ inches. Their teeth were excellent, partly because the Romans used honey instead of refined sugar as their sweetener. About 20 percent of the adults had suffered a trauma that had left a mark—but Roman medicine was able to heal them.

Bisel found a level of lead in their bones that was about the same as in the bones of contemporary Greeks. This finding has helped discredit a theory that the decline and fall of the Roman Empire had been caused by lead poisoning from the Romans' wine, which was prepared in lead vessels and often sweetened with lead acetate.

Icelandic volcanologist Haraldur Sigurdsson received Society funding to study the eruption that had destroyed Herculaneum. In the first 11 hours of the eruption, he found, Mount Vesuvius hurled a column of pumice 12 miles into the sky. About midnight on August 24th, the column collapsed for the first time, sending a superheated avalanche of gases, pumice, and rocks down the mountainside. It split into two parts, a fast-moving surge that blasted through Herculaneum, and a slower, ground-hugging pyroclastic flow that buried the city. The eruption was ten times the size of the Mount St. Helens explosion of 1980, according to Dr. Sigurdsson. Some of the wood in Herculaneum was heated to 750°F.

New World archaeology as well as Old has received Society backing.

DONALD A. FREY/INA

Going up: Amphorae from a Byzantine ship sunk off Turkey 1,300 years ago ascend, buoyed by a cloth balloon. Bass pioneered such procedures.

Among the Native American cultures of the southwestern United States, Society-funded work began in 1920 with the support of Neil M. Judd at Pueblo Bonito in New Mexico's Chaco Canyon.

The Anasazi—"the ancient ones"—lived here about 2,000 years ago, hunting and gathering, gradually settling down to become sedentary corn farmers. They built multifamily structures and laced their territory with hundreds of miles of roads. To water their cornfields, they built ingenious irrigation devices.

Though the Anasazi were never a

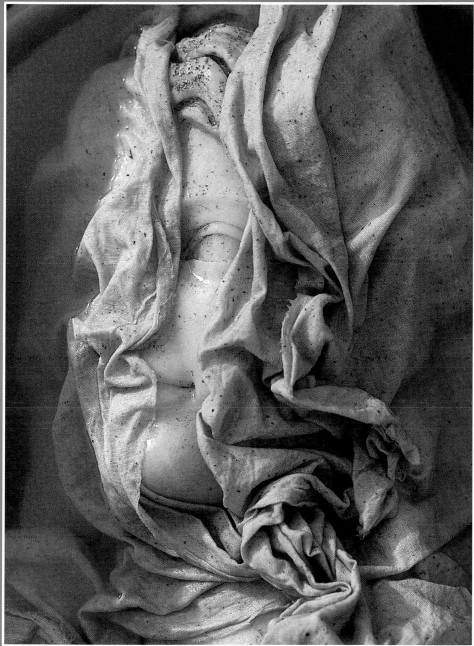

Aphrodisias

"I have selected this one city from all of Asia as my own," wrote future Emperor Augustus of Aphrodisias, a Greco-Roman metropolis that flourished from the second century B.C. to the sixth century A.D. Battered by earthquakes in the fourth and seventh centuries, the city, in present- day Turkey, lay abandoned for hundreds of years. In 1966, NGS began funding excavation there. Digs revealed an 8,000-seat theater (opposite) and dazzling sculpture, including an Aphrodite (above), here soaking in water to leach impurities. Kenan T. Erim, the dig's director, called the marble sculptures "extraordinary...enduring."

O. LOUIS MAZZATENTA/NATIONAL GEOGRAPHIC STAFF (BOTH)

single tribe or language group, they shared certain characteristics—a distinctive pottery, pueblo homes, community living, and similar religious practices.

About a thousand years ago, Anasazi in Chaco Canyon began building their masterpiece—Pueblo Bonito, "beautiful village." Within a few years, it contained more than a hundred rooms and rose three stories. Then construction halted. A hundred years later it began again during an era of grandeur now known as the "Chaco phenomenon." New construction—and renovation of old—took place for 130 years. Pueblo Bonito grew to 5 stories and 650 rooms. (Nothing larger would be built in what is now the United States until the 1870s.)

Then the Anasazi mysteriously vanished into the mists of time.

A number of Society grants have focused on various aspects of the Anasazi culture. A grant in 1976 to Ray A. Williamson of St. John's College in Annapolis, Maryland, helped him investigate the Hovenweep towers, a series of rock monuments built some 800 years ago by the Anasazi along what is now the Utah-Colorado border. They perched precariously on the edges of mesas or atop large boulders and rose as high as 19 feet. They were constructed of dressed sandstone blocks chinked with stone chips and mortared with mud. Their purpose had long been a mystery. Were they astronomical

Ghostly blurs in the camera's eye recall Herculaneum's former citizens. This, the town's main street, once was lined with busy shops. A modern suburb of Naples overlooks the ruins.

observatories or signal towers? Probably both, Williamson surmised.

With a grant in 1981, Paul S. Martin of the University of Arizona reconstructed the history of vegetation in Chaco Canyon, largely by studying the middens of pack rats, some of them thousands of years old. The animals mark their caches with urine, which, when it dries, preserves the plant debris and other things they collect in an amberlike resin that can survive for millennia.

The Anasazi drew upon an extensive piñon-juniper woodland for their firewood, and the timing of its disappearance likely played a role in their civilization's end. "A major reduction in the Chaco woodland," Martin found, "is registered only recently, between 1,200 and 500 years ago, and most likely due to human impact rather than climate." The tendency of the Chacoans to inhabit a site only briefly probably indicates that as the population grew, the supply of firewood in an area was depleted.

In 1984, a grant to archaeologist E. Charles Adams allowed him to analyze artifacts from Sand Canyon Pueblo, a 13th-century Anasazi ceremonial center near Mesa Verde in Colorado. And in 1986, Jonathan Haas, of the School of American Research in Santa Fe, used Society funds to survey rock-shelters in the Tsegi Canyon system of northeastern est treasuries of art and architecture in all the Americas," according to George E. Stuart, Society staff archaeologist and member of the committee.

With a grant in the late 1980s, archaeologists William L. Fash, Jr., and Ricardo Agurcia Fasquelle, co-directors of the Copán Acropolis Archaeological Project, uncovered a royal Maya tomb.

The Maya often built one structure atop an older one, partially destroying the previous edifice, then covering it with rubble. An archaeology student, tunneling into a pyramid at Copán, was following a buried stairway upward when he came upon a column, a ceramic offering, and a vaulted chamber filled with rubble. Beneath the rubble lay a capstone, and on June 4, 1989, it was lifted to reveal the inside of a tomb. There were remnants of red plaster, scattered pottery vessels, and bones. Analysis of the bones and bone fragments indicated they were those of a man between 35 and 40 who had lived a life of ease—perhaps a member of royalty. A young boy's skeleton was found nearby. His teeth indicated he was a commoner; probably he had been sacrificed to accompany the royal personage on his trip to the next world.

Pottery found nearby gave more clues. One pot was filled with red pigment, the property of a scribe; another was decorated with an image of the patron god of scribes. Fash and Agurcia knew that the younger sons of kings were often trained in this skill, so they concluded that the royal personage was a royal scribe, the son of Copán's greatest king—Smoke Imix.

The following year the two men reported another remarkable find in nearby Structure 16: a temple within a pyramid within a pyramid. Painted bright red and decorated with elaborate carvings of figures from the complex Maya cosmology, the temple

Bronze African slave boys, found in 1933 at Herculaneum, dance to rhythms long since stilled.

Arizona, trying to determine why some shelters were utilized by the Anasazi at certain times and not at others.

Over the decades, the ruins of the Maya civilization far to the south in Middle America have acted as magnets to archaeologists. The Committee for Research and Exploration has funded more than a hundred projects in the Maya world. The Classic Maya Period—which fell roughly between A.D. 250 and 900—produced magnificent sites, including the masterpiece city of Copán in western Honduras, "one of the great-

ALBERT MOLDVAY

Wetherill Mesa

An archaeological treasure—a bowl made by the mysterious builders of pueblos in the Southwest known as the Anasazi—sees the light of day at Wetherill Mesa in Colorado's Mesa Verde National Park. In 1958 the Society began a project here with the National Park Service, funded in part by a $320,000 grant. Park Service archaeologist Douglas Osborne wrote: "Thus we were able to bring to bear many varied fields of study—from dendrochronology (tree-ring dating)...to archeoentomology (study of ancient insects)." The five-year effort contributed to a deeper grasp of life in pre-Columbian America.

had been carefully "mummified"—encased in coarse, thick plaster, then buried in rubble. To the Maya, evidently, buildings died just as humans did and often were accorded the same reverential burial.

And in a crude niche made of small stones in its western room the archaeologists found "the most spectacular ceremonial offering ever unearthed at Copán": three chert knives, a jade bead, a stingray spine, three spiny oyster shells, and many small shark vertebrae. But most exciting were nine "eccentric flints"—intricate sculptures of human profiles made by carefully flaking chips off pieces of chert. The craftsmanship was magnificent, as fine as anything in the Americas. Archaeologists are still puzzled by the flints' purpose: They may once have adorned the shafts of ceremonial staffs and perhaps represent the nine divine Maya lords of the night.

At about the same time the Maya civilization was flourishing, a little-known society on the dry coastal plains of northern Peru was beginning its decline. The pre-Inca Moche had managed to prosper in the arid and desolate valleys of the region. Their complex irrigation system drew water from high in the distant Andes, and they built large mounds, called *huacas*, of millions of adobe bricks. These were used as ceremonial centers and sometimes as mausoleums. The civilization flourished from A.D. 100 to 700. At its height, there were some 50,000 Moche.

Three Society grants have helped archaeologists study the Moche. Mary Eubanks Dunn, of Southern Methodist University, received a grant "in support of an investigation of the ceramic evi-

dence for the spread of prehistoric races of maize in Peru." The Moche used actual ears of corn to create molds, which they then used to depict maize in relief on their pottery. As the molds duplicated "in every detail" the botanical specimens, much can be learned of Moche agriculture by studying their pottery. Dr. Dunn identified 13 races of maize on 26 Moche jars.

And in 1987, Society funds arrived

in Peru just in time to prevent a calamitous act of looting. Walter Alva, director of the Brüning Archaeological Museum in Lambayeque, Peru, received a call from the local police one night in February 1987, asking him to examine some Moche artifacts recovered from the home of a local *huaquero*, or grave robber. For decades, local Peruvians had supplemented their meager incomes by digging in unguarded Moche sites; the

Pueblo Bonito, once home to hundreds of Anasazi, pocks a dry plain of New Mexico. In the 1920s grantee Neil M. Judd hired Navajo and Zuni workers to dig from a tent camp here.

results of their efforts are in private collections and museums all over the world. These artifacts were looted by tunneling into a large huaca near the town of Sipán. The huaqueros had

WILLIAM BELKNAP; DEWITT JONES (OPPOSITE)

penetrated a tomb "of unprecedented magnificence," Dr. Alva would later say.

Alva recognized the importance of the recovered artifacts and appealed for help in protecting the huaca before more looting occurred. Christopher B. Donnan, director of the Museum of Cultural History at UCLA—author of *Moche Art of Peru* and one of the world's leading authorities on Moche art—came to the research committee in Washington with slides of the recovered artifacts and requested emergency funding. Guards needed to be hired immediately to protect the site.

Meanwhile, back in Peru, Alva was living in a tent at the site trying to protect it from the bold and determined huaqueros. The local police had killed one of them during a raid, and his angry relatives were vowing revenge. Gunfire disturbed the hot Peruvian nights.

Astonishingly, the shovels of the huaqueros had come within a few feet of an even richer tomb that Alva uncovered several months later. Alva called the occupant of this tomb the "Lord of Sipán." By the time he had completed excavating the tomb, the treasures included "a solid gold headdress two feet across, a gold face mask, a gold knife, multiple strands of large gold and silver beads, a beautifully crafted rattle hammered from sheet gold…gold bells showing a deity engaged in severing human heads…and exquisite gold-and-turquoise ear ornaments."

He had had company on his journey to the next life. Two women, about 20 years old, were buried at his head and

Cliff Palace attests to the Anasazi's skill both as architects and as builders. Square rooms were for living; round kivas, for ceremonies.

feet. Two men, about 40, one buried with a dog, flanked his coffin. And a young man, dubbed "the guardian," lay a few feet above him. Several of the retinue had feet missing, perhaps amputated to keep them loyal even in death.

With the Lord of Sipán in his coffin was a dazzling array of artifacts and riches. Feather ornaments lay in groups above and below the body. Fabric banners with gilded copper platelets covered it. Eleven pectorals (chest coverings) of shell and copper beads appeared in layers. A gilded copper headdress rested atop a textile headband used to secure it. The lord's face, ears, neck, and chest were festooned with gold, silver, and copper ornaments. Turquoise-and-gold-bead bracelets clasped his forearms. Gold and copper ingots lay on his hands, and the right hand held a gold rattle; the left, a silver knife. Seashells had been placed at his copper-sandal-clad feet. Beneath him was a massive gold headdress, and beneath that were crescent-shaped gold bells and a small gold headdress ornament. Three shrouds enfolded all.

An artist's imagination peoples an excavated Maya ball court in Copán (right) with players observed by a powerful and divine ruler-spectator. To the Maya, the ball game was both metaphor and sport, a tussle between men and mythical beings. Copán, in the highlands of Honduras, flourished in the eighth century.

KENNETH GARRETT

H. TOM HALL

It was the richest cache of pre-Columbian artifacts ever scientifically excavated in the Americas. Dr. Donnan wrote, "Overall, the Sipán Project has been extraordinarily successful and is already a landmark in New World archaeology. Never before has it been possible to excavate such a wealth of artifacts and scientific information regarding the elite class within a major Pre-Columbian civilization. Much of the success of this research is directly due to the generous support of the National Geographic Society."

Nearer to home, Society grants have shed light on the colonial history of the United States.

There were times when it must have been terrifying to be a colonist. For a handful of colonists in the British settlement of Wolstenholme Towne in Virginia, the end came unexpectedly. While sharing a seemingly congenial breakfast with Indians of the Powhatan chiefdom, the settlers were taken by surprise when the Indians suddenly attacked.

Ten miles east of Jamestown,

Wolstenholme Towne was the administrative center of Martin's Hundred, home to clerks and administrators. The houses all extended outward from a fort-like stockade where Governor William Harwood lived.

The attack by the Powhatan Indians came on a wintry Friday morning—March 22, 1622—and when it was over, 58 settlers were dead and the rest were thoroughly demoralized. The three-year-old settlement was a charred ruin. New settlers and supplies arrived from London to reinforce the survivors, but the tiny settlement never regained a successful foothold. The years came and went, and the decades, and the centuries—and gradually all trace of Wolstenholme Towne vanished.

In 1970, Ivor Noël Hume, director of the department of archaeology at the Colonial Williamsburg Foundation, was organizing the exploration of 500 acres of land—an 18th-century plantation named Carter's Grove—that had been newly donated to Colonial

Williamsburg. Everyone had forgotten that it had grown up where Wolstenholme Towne once stood.

"We were totally unprepared for what we found," Noël Hume later wrote. Instead of 18th-century artifacts from Carter's Grove, his workers' shovels and trowels were turning up pottery, pipes, and postholes from a hundred years earlier. Their site obviously wasn't 18th-century; it was 17th.

Postholes yield data to an archaeologist in two ways: In a hole's outer

Gullied by erosion, ancient *huacas*—adobe brick mounds—rise from Peru's coastal plain. The Moche built the mounds more than 1,700 years ago to entomb nobility. Archaeologists uncovered vast riches buried here (top), including a gold-and-turquoise ear ornament (above).

perimeter, where earth was filled in around the post, the most recent artifact gives a date after which the post was erected; in the post mold, where the post

Accompanied even by his dog, a royal Moche had plenty of companions on his trip to the next world. Society funds, rushed to Peru, helped pay guards to protect the site from looters.

itself stood, the most recent artifact gives a date after which the post had disappeared. Many of Wolstenholme's postholes contained ashes, evidence that the town had suffered a fiery end.

The excavation of Wolstenholme took place over several years in the late 1970s. As it proceeded, a picture of life in early colonial America gradually emerged. Like detectives, Noël Hume and his team pieced together fragments of evidence to reconstruct the colonists' settlement and lives.

A number of graves had been dug simultaneously, suggesting that those buried there had died of disease, many in their youth. Some artifacts—glass bottles, earthenware flasks from Spain, marbleized slipware plates from Italy, stoneware bottles and jugs from the Rhineland, tin-glazed ware from England and Holland—may have belonged to Governor Harwood himself. The remains of a still indicated the colonists made medicinal brews and liquor.

But most interesting to Noël Hume was the layout of the settlement, traced through dozens of postholes. It is the earliest partial layout of a British town yet found in America, and closely resembles the bawn-protected villages of colonial Ireland.

In death, layers of finery wrap a Moche king in a cocoon of riches (above, left). As archaeologists dug, they found him lying amid feather trim, fabric banners, shell pectorals, gold and silver ornaments, turquoise bracelets, and seashells.

But what of the living? While archaeologists concern themselves with the dead, other anthropologists seek out the quick.

Over the decades, hundreds of National Geographic grants have gone to those anthropologists who, with their notebooks and tape recorders, nose their way into villages and kinship groups around the world, always asking questions. Society grant recipients have investigated the Ayoreo Indians of Bolivia and Paraguay, the Dani people of Indonesia, Australia's Aborigines, and the Barabaig people of Tanzania, among hundreds of others.

One of the most unusual research grants went to a 73-year-old Benedictine nun, Sister Mary Inez Hilger, to study the Ainu—enigmatic aboriginal inhabitants of Japan's Hokkaido island.

The Ainu had long puzzled scholars. To some anthropologists, their round eyes and abundant hair—which led to the pejorative "hairy Ainu"

Nomads camp where Genghis Khan rode. For six months grantees Melvyn Goldstein and Cynthia Beall lived here, in the harsh mountains of western Mongolia, studying the effects of the collapse of communism on the herders.

nickname—seemed evidence of Caucasian ancestry. Other researchers sought a link between the Ainu and Australia's Aborigines. Now almost totally assimilated into the Japanese population, the Ainu may in fact have been a separate people, who had lived on Hokkaido for at least 7,000 years.

"I wanted to anticipate the staggering loss to ethnology that the passing of the present generation of Ainu grandparents will represent," Sister Inez wrote. In the mid-sixties, before the Ainu had largely disappeared, Sister Inez lived among them for eight months, charming them with her simplicity and courtesy and impressing them with her vigor. At an early meeting, the Ainu women rose, "and each stroked my face, whimpering with joy, then tested with both hands the muscles in my forearms. How old was I? Seventy-three. 'Unbelievable!' they chorused. 'Why, you have the strength of a much younger woman.'"

They were touched by her interest in their lives. "'Oh, we are very glad you have come, Holy Woman, to put it all down on paper—to record the way we Ainu used to do things!'"

Few traditional Ainu remain today. Of the approximately 24,000 persons on Hokkaido who are considered Ainu, a handful are purebloods; and their language and religion are disappearing. Sister Inez died in 1977.

Another group of people, primitive

Reluctant bronco tries to throw its Mongolian cowboy. Each household keeps a horse or two tethered to the family *ger*, or tent, while the main herd of 50 or so roams free.

Mongolian nomad women prepare *bordzig*, a deep-fried pastry. Their lives until recently were regulated by Soviet-style communism; now they struggle to adapt to new freedoms.

CYNTHIA BEALL & MELVYN GOLDSTEIN

by modern standards but fiercely protective of their traditional life-style, are maintaining their identity in the face of 20th-century pressures in Tibet. Some 400,000 to 500,000 nomads roam the high Himalayan pastures of the Chang Tang area, herding yaks, sheep, goats, and horses. One group—the Phala nomads—live in an area about 300 miles northwest of Lhasa. Some 260 strong, they move among pastures that are between 16,000 and 17,500 feet high, which makes them the highest resident native population known in the world.

In the late 1960s, the Chinese forced the nomads into communes, then reversed themselves in 1980 and allowed the people to reconstruct their tradi-

tional lives. Melvyn Goldstein and Cynthia Beall, Society grant recipients who have also studied Mongolian nomads, were the first Western anthropologists allowed to do long-term fieldwork in Tibet. They spent 16 months among the Phala nomads, trailing along on their migrations, riding yaks, drinking tea, and asking questions. "The nomads continue to flourish," they wrote, "because they have no competitors. Even with modern technology farmers cannot grow crops in the extreme high altitude and bitter climate of the Chang Tang. If there were no nomads on the high plateau, it would revert to wild animals, not to other humans."

The nomads feel their way of life is

In a Sphinx-like stance, a pack camel is prepared for another trip. Nomadic herders represent some two-fifths of Mongolia's 2.2 million people and live among peaks that reach 14,000 feet.

MELVYN GOLDSTEIN

easier than that of farmers. "'Look,' explained one, 'it is obvious that we have a very easy life. The grass grows by itself, the animals reproduce by themselves, they give milk and meat without our doing anything. So how can you say our way of life is hard?'" The yak is their most precious animal, so vital to their economy that the nomads' name for the beast is *nor,* meaning "wealth."

The Phala have achieved a rough balance with their environment. Their pastures are not overgrazed, though the Chinese government has instituted limits on the number of animals per person in some areas and has forced periodic reductions in herd size in others.

"Preserving the unique environ-ment of the Chang Tang is not only a Chinese but also a world concern," wrote Goldstein and Beall, "and protec-tion of the indigenous people who reside there is equally important."

Despite the interference of the Chinese government, "for now, and for the foreseeable future, the nomadic pastoral way of life is alive and well on the Chang Tang, and all of us are richer for it."

Richer, too, is *our* world for the understanding of past cultures and different societies that the study of anthropology gives us. Peoples of the past—silenced by eternity—speak again through the work of scientists. This is how we lived, the people say. This was the world as *we* knew it.

Efe Clans of Zaire

Deep in the Ituri rain forest of Zaire, an Efe hunter, one of the African people known as Pygmies, takes aim. In 1980, with Society support, UCLA anthropologist Robert C. Bailey lived with one of the semi-nomadic Efe clans. He hoped to determine the extent to which the Efe subsisted by hunting and gathering, as opposed to trading with the more settled Lese people who lived nearby in semipermanent villages. "Meat, honey, a few gathered fruits, and building materials are brought to the villages to exchange for cultivated foods and material goods," Dr. Bailey wrote. To study the Efe diet, Bailey weighed all food entering and leaving their camps on 33 randomly selected days between March 1981 and March 1982; to keep track of their work activities, interactions, association patterns, and other aspects of their social behavior, he collected 376 hours of observations on 16 Efe men and found they devoted 52.3 percent of their time to subsistence activities. Efe women "largely specialized their subsistence activities around the Lese villages and gardens," he wrote. The Efe subsisted largely on cassava, nuts, rice, wild plants, fish, honey, and meat. The forest supplied 36.5 percent of their diet, and the gardens of the Lese 63.5 percent. "The forest, as lush as it appears, does not have the density and abundance of edible resources to sustain human foragers for long periods," Bailey concluded. A second grant in 1991 allowed Dr. Bailey to return to Zaire to continue his research in the Ituri forest.

JOSÉ AZEL/AURORA

Observing Animals
in the Wild

By Jennifer C. Urquhart

High above, in a large nest in the leafy branches of a *mgwiza* tree, an old chimpanzee lay dying. Below, on the forest floor, Jane Goodall kept vigil.

"I didn't want her to be completely

BOB CAMPBELL (PRECEDING PAGES); HUGO VAN LAWICK (BOTH)

Palm-shaded Old Camp served Jane Goodall during her early years at Gombe Stream Reserve. Homely old Flo (opposite) provided much insight into the chimp mother-offspring bond.

Preceding Pages: In the company of two gorillas, Dian Fossey reads notes in Rwanda's Virunga Mountains.

alone," Goodall said of the old friend she called Melissa. Together, over the years, they had wandered from one food patch to another. Goodall would wait and watch while Melissa rested or paused to groom with an offspring. After more than 30 years observing chimpanzees in what is now Tanzania's

Gombe National Park, Goodall would call this deathwatch beneath the mgwiza tree her most poignant memory.

National Geographic Society research grants have supported the work of Goodall and other brave and adventurous investigators in observing animals in such isolated corners of Africa. Other researchers have ventured into the steaming rain forests of Borneo, home to the reclusive orangutan; traversed barren stretches of the high Arctic, domain of the white wolf; traveled to remote areas of southern Chile in search of guanacos; penetrated caves inhabited by millions of bats; and climbed high into Rwanda's rain forest to observe rare mountain gorillas. They have carried out painstaking studies to grasp how animals interact with one another and their environment—and to ponder why. They have endured hardships. They have come up with dazzling discoveries. And often these students of behavior have been transformed into dedicated advocates for the survival and well-being of their subjects.

"Man has always been interested in other animals," wrote Leonard Carmichael, chairman of the research committee from 1960 to 1973, "for one very basic reason: He wants to eat them.... Successful hunters and fishermen are always animal behaviorists."

That early humans found spiritual connection with animals is evinced in prehistoric cave paintings and early totemic symbolism. Now other interests motivate us: We observe animals to learn about our own biological makeup and to discover parallels with human behavior.

"We recognize," noted Carmichael, "many traits that we share with our

David Greybeard, here cadging bananas from Goodall, "opened my first window onto the chimpanzee's world," she says. She watched him eat meat and use a stem tool to fish for termites—observations that helped her gain NGS support. With son Flint in attendance, Flo and another female (right) hunt their own termites.

nonhuman companions in the living world: social bonds, maternal care, aggression, submission, and ownership of territory; even, alas, deception and greed." And, in learning about animals in their own world, we perhaps will "learn more than a little about how we live in ours."

In the early 20th century the study of wild animal behavior tended toward anecdotal commentary by naturalists. By mid-century, however, researchers were using modern methods and technology. Observations became more precise as scientists pursued the new field of ethology, the scientific study of animal behavior.

Charles H. Southwick, zoologist and member of the research committee since 1979, points to the importance of

the work Society grants have funded. "Back in Leonard Carmichael's day, which was in the early days of field primatology, with Jane Goodall, Dian Fossey, and George Schaller's first studies, everything was pioneering research. Goodall did the first real study on chimpanzee natural behavior. Though not specifically backed by the Society, Schaller's was the first in-depth mountain gorilla study. Now the work has progressed to a much higher degree of sophistication and analysis."

In 1960, Goodall, a young English girl without a university degree, landed on the shores of Lake Tanganyika at the Gombe Stream Reserve to study a group of some 150 wild chimpanzees. Her mentor was Louis S. B. Leakey, and at the time his agenda differed slightly

MICHAEL K. NICHOLS/MAGNUM; DIAN FOSSEY (OPPOSITE)

Goodall now fights for the humane treatment of chimps in captivity. Here, in the Canary Islands, she holds one of a group of "beach chimps" she described as drugged and sick.

Opposite: Digit, Dian Fossey's friend, was killed by poachers in 1977.

from hers. He thought a good look at the way of life of chimpanzees might offer insight into the behavior of early man.

Jane Goodall became the first of "Leakey's Angels"—the women primatologists who pioneered the field. She would eventually earn her academic credentials at Cambridge University, but why had Leakey taken her on then?

"Louis Leakey felt that women were better observers and more patient," Goodall told me. "I don't think we are better observers, but patience is built into our genes as a characteristic, over the eons of evolution, because women have to be patient to be good mothers. Even more important, women have had to learn to understand the wants and expressions of nonverbal beings—the babies in their families before they talk."

At first Goodall could not get any closer to the chimpanzees than 500 yards, then 100 yards. Day after day she persistently trailed her subjects, often peering through binoculars from a high vantage called the Peak and filling little notebooks with commentary. Sometimes she took a kettle, a little coffee and sugar, and a blanket and waited through the night to watch the chimpanzees rise in the morning. From the Peak she first saw a male she called David Greybeard share an infant bush pig with a female chimpanzee, and she learned that the apes were hunters and meat eaters. And nearby, in October 1960, "I had watched David Greybeard, along with his friend Goliath, fishing for termites with stems of grass," Goodall later wrote. David picked a wide stem and trimmed it so that it could be poked into the narrow passage in the termite mound. "Not only was he using the grass as a tool—he was, by modifying it to suit a special purpose, actually showing the crude beginnings of tool-*making*."

It was a lucky stroke. Except for those observations, Goodall's studies might have ended right there; her small grant was running out. With this evidence of tool using and meat consumption, she said, "Dr. Leakey could go to the Geographic and say 'look, this young English girl with no training actually is finding something.' So then the Geographic came in and they really supported everything I did for the next six years or so." And so began the Society's long tradition of promoting primate field research.

Goodall's ape companions in the forest were a lively cast of characters, exhibiting great individuality. Her myriad

STUART PERLMETER

adventures would become legendary through NATIONAL GEOGRAPHIC magazine articles and TV specials.

Goodall's observations revealed a complex kaleidoscope of daily interactions in a close-knit society led by a dominant alpha male. She observed the highly socialized primates close up, building nests, communicating vocally, and exchanging such affectionate gestures as hugs and greeting kisses and pats of reassurance. These gestures are so humanlike that Goodall believes they either have a common origin with human gestures or have evolved along closely parallel lines.

She would observe and name the madcap "rain dance" performed by the males, usually in a storm, as they charged downhill flailing branches and calling wildly. Turmoil increased when adult males jockeyed for dominance.

From a female named Flo and her offspring, Goodall learned about the female hierarchy. She was particularly struck by the closeness of mothers and daughters and by how young females imitated their mothers' nurturing styles, even practicing on infant siblings. A sociable, high-ranking mother like Flo had well-adjusted, high-ranking progeny. The offspring of shy or high-strung mothers tended to be less successful.

In the first few years Gombe seemed a peaceable kingdom. Then between 1974 and 1977 came what Jane Goodall has called the "darkest years in Gombe's history." She observed infanticide, cannibalism, and extreme violence between chimpanzee communities as the Kas-

Africa's Virunga Mountains, Fossey fought constantly against poachers. Here, in 1967, she escapes the war-torn Congo by moving camp to Mount Visoke in neighboring Rwanda.

ALAN ROOT

akela group annihilated the splinter Kahama group.

"For so many years I had believed that chimpanzees, while showing uncanny similarities to humans in many ways, were, by and large, rather 'nicer' than us," she said. Now she saw that "they could be just as brutal, that they had a dark side to their nature. And it hurt." Goodall maintains, however, that chimpanzees, unlike humans, are incapable of deliberate cruelty.

In recent years, Jane Goodall has turned much of her work at Gombe over to Tanzanians. She now travels tirelessly to promote conservation of wild chimpanzees and humane treatment of those in captivity. She writes with pride of the "harvest" of her work, "the understanding that has come from long hours spent with our closest living relatives."

It is a far cry, though not so far on the map, from the savanna-woodland world of boisterous chimpanzees to the fog-bound forest of the mountain gorilla, where, in 1967, the second of "Leakey's Angels," Dian Fossey, beat her way.

Like Goodall, Fossey had no formal training and was obsessed by her dream of Africa. She wanted to work with animals. Leakey obliged the Californian by sending her into the Virunga Mountains bordering Rwanda and Zaire. There, with the help of NGS grants, she would earn her academic credentials, also through Cambridge University, and spend the better part of two decades in pursuit of the shy, elusive apes. She continued work begun a decade earlier by

field biologist George B. Schaller, who had noted that "the literature on free-living gorillas is embarrassingly voluminous, considering the paucity of accurate information it contains."

As with Goodall, it fell to Fossey to develop techniques that allowed her to observe the animals. To habituate the apes, she acted like a gorilla, imitating their hoot, grunt, and belch vocalizations. She munched the same vegetation and displayed submission gestures. Eventually accepted, she was able to observe a usually gentle, well-ordered domesticity, under the benevolent eye of a silverback—a mature male—as leader.

Fossey weathered political upheaval, civil war, and the vicious killing by poachers of several of the adult gorillas, including the silverback she'd named Uncle Bert and the one she unabashedly called "my beloved Digit." Until her brutal murder in 1985, in her camp at the Karisoke Research Centre in Rwanda's Parc National des Volcans, she filled in gaps in the knowledge of these rare primates. She refuted the old King Kong mythology that characterized gorillas as dangerous. Violent chest beating, the stuff of grade-B movies, was mostly bluff—unless, of course, the family group was in some way threatened (though later in her studies she discovered a violent side to gorilla behavior—fierce sexual conflict and occasional infanticide of a rival male's progeny).

She also pursued with passion her crusade—which perhaps precipitated her violent end, probably at the hands of vengeful poachers—to protect what had become her adored, and increasingly endangered, gorillas. Though she paid with her life for her commitment to Digit and the other apes of the rain forest and was laid to rest there on her mountain, Fossey lives on in her studies. Her work and her death opened the world's eyes to the animals' plight and inspired the

ROD BRINDAMOUR; DENIS TACKETT/TOM STACK & ASSOCIATES (OPPOSITE)

Strong fingers secure the grip of a subadult male orangutan (opposite). Biruté Galdikas has studied orangutans, most arboreal of the great apes, for 20 years in Borneo. One of her ex-captives (above) tries on a milk pan.

Mountain Gorilla Project, which continues to document the story of gorillas, to protect them from poachers, and to educate the local people about their unique zoological treasure.

To the jungles of Borneo, in 1971, Leakey sent the third of his women primatologists, Biruté Galdikas, a Canadian graduate student living in California.

Life for Galdikas since then, in the swampy rain forest of Tanjung Puting, in the southwestern part of Indonesian Borneo, has been somewhat schizophrenic. From the beginning her responsibilities were dual. Her first aim, with Society backing, was to study the social behavior and the ecology of the orangutan, known for its solitary habits. Her second goal was to set up a sort of halfway house for wild-born, ex-captive were using their high ape intelligence to maximum capacity just thinking up new ways of driving me crazy.

"The orangutan is the one ape that never left the Garden of Eden," said Galdikas. As we learn why this great ape evolved so differently from other apes, she feels, we may learn a great deal about the evolution of human society.

Why did orangutans never develop the social skills and interdependence of other apes? The answer may be that they never needed to, or, perhaps, that they could not have survived as fruit eaters in the rain forest if they had turned sociable. The orangutan's solitary ways seem suited to the rain forest, where trees bear fruit at erratic intervals. If the animals congregated to feed off a single tree, it would be stripped and might not fruit again easily. In documenting their vegetable and fruit diet, Galdikas has learned how orangutans have adapted to and furthered, through seed dispersal, the great biodiversity of the tropical rain forest. "In my study area," she said, "they eat 400 different types of food. The animals seem to have an uncanny memory of not only where a particular tree is, but when it is due to produce fruit." They bee-line through jungle to trees they cannot see.

Through long days of tedious work, pushing miles through the forest often in waist-deep water, Galdikas has filled in a picture of the life of the red ape, as the orangutan is also called because of its bright, punkish-wild hair.

"Orangutans raise very few offspring, but they raise them to maturity," Galdikas told me. Despite that success, their life cycle leaves them surprisingly vulnerable to extinction. Their birth interval is the longest of any mammal: A female gives birth only once every eight

A playful ex-captive orangutan chews a stem. In her 14-square-mile study area alone, Galdikas has found that the apes consume 400 kinds of food.

young orangutans for reintroduction into the forest. Half the time she could hardly find her subjects; the other half she couldn't escape them.

In the forest "they are silent creatures," Galdikas said. To locate feeding orangutans a hundred feet up in the canopy, she had to rely on bits of food debris pitter-pattering to the forest floor. In camp, however, unruly young primates clung to her and wreaked havoc. On occasion, after a long day following wild orangutans for miles, she would be rewarded with chaos in camp: a young orangutan looking "like the Abominable Snowman in a blizzard," aswirl in white kapok from eviscerated bedding; the garden destroyed; books chewed; toddler-proof medicine bottles opened; socks in the coffee. "I was sometimes convinced," Galdikas said, "that they

years or so, she has discovered, and does not have her first offspring until the age of 15 or 16. "If you demolish or decimate an orangutan population in the wild, that population isn't going to bounce back very quickly."

She has observed combat between adult males never seen by scientists before. But that combat, she has concluded, is only common when an adult male is consorting with a female. Other-

Surrogate-motherhood for Galdikas includes a toe-tickling session with two young orangutans. Logging often leaves the infants orphaned.

wise males are likely to retreat from conflict. Only occasionally does Galdikas have intimate encounters with her subjects. But once, she told me, "a wild adolescent female suddenly came down from the canopy, very low, almost on a

level with me, and just looked into my eyes, almost drinking me in, as though trying to ascertain who I was or what kind of being. I scarcely dared breathe because I didn't want to break the fragility of the moment, because it was so rare."

No primate behaves more differently from the orangutan than the baboon. In 1972, anthropology graduate student Shirley C. Strum went to Kekopey Ranch in central Kenya to study the baboons that range the cliff-riddled scrublands there. Later, Society research grants would support her work.

At that time, one established theory of baboon society held that a troop was rigidly organized under the leadership of a core of adult males, which gained power through aggressive competition. Strum's studies would turn that interpretation upside down: Not only did females count, but males had other ways besides aggression and dominance to get what they wanted. The animals rely on a "complex network of relationships," she writes, "on social skill and the timely use of social maneuvers to achieve their goals."

She recalls the early days when an adult male called Ray joined the Pumphouse Gang, as one troop was designated because of the pumping station on its home range. She and Ray arrived about the same time.

"We both sought acceptance and we both—at first—were viewed askance." She wondered then if he would accost a female or challenge the top male by baring his fearsome canines and by other aggressive behavior. But no, like Strum he sat quietly watching. Then Ray sought the company of a female known as Naomi and spent months cultivating her and other females. Ultimately Ray negotiated his way into Pumphouse society. And with Ray, Strum began to unravel the complexities of the males'

SHIRLEY C. STRUM; TIM W. RANSOM (OPPOSITE)

A radio collar helps Shirley Strum track the Pumphouse Gang during the baboon troop's translocation. Her studies shed light on the species' male-female roles. A juvenile (opposite) tugs at a balking infant.

position in the social structure. "Every one of the seven adult males had at least one female friend," she noticed. "The cementing of that first friendship was a new male's key to group acceptance." There was, of course, the core close-knit family unit of mother and offspring. Upon closer scrutiny another important relationship emerged: friendship. Unrelated baboons seem to "like simply to be together, sitting, resting, sleeping,

Mom's rumble seat makes a perfect perch for a soon-to-be-weaned five-month-old. Strum's experience in moving baboons may help relocate primates that are endangered.

grooming, and often moving near one another when the troop foraged," Strum reported in NATIONAL GEOGRAPHIC. These friendships developed between females, between males and females even outside mating cycles, but never between adult males.

After more than a decade of close observation, Strum's Pumphouse Gang and the other troops were becoming seriously threatened by conversion of rangeland to farms. Farmers did not take kindly to baboons raiding their crops, and some baboons were shot.

Strum tried a daring experiment—translocating the baboons to a less populated area. "I felt sure that the animals would have at least a fifty-fifty chance if I did move them, and faced certain death if I did not." With Society backing and with tremendous logistical planning, in September 1984, Strum and her crew trapped and moved three troops of baboons to a much more arid site 150 miles to the northeast.

Of the first release of the animals there, Strum wrote, "I don't know which touched me more, the mournful *wahoo* of the captives as their friends and relatives…scattered from the release site or the reassuring embraces of the reunited troop when we uncaged the males."

Baboons are known to be opportunistic and adaptable. The translocation posed the real test. Despite the complications posed by a severe drought, "the baboons have done really well," Strum says. "They learned how to eat foods they'd never seen before, including foods critical to their survival in the dry season."

Like humans, animals communicate in various ways through body language and vocalization. Animal behaviorists yearn to read the subtle signals that their subjects use.

Everyone recognizes the high-pitched screams and trumpetings of an elephant. Elephants also make deep rumbling sounds that hunters and biologists once wrote off as digestive activity.

A lifelong interest in nature and a background in music lured Katharine Payne into the field of animal vocalization. For many years she had pursued the haunting songs of whales, especially of the humpbacks, and had come up with extraordinary findings about the intricacies of whale communication. Then, in 1984, she decided that she'd like to work with the largest terrestrial mammal, the elephant.

Trap-jaw Ants

To defend home or capture dinner, a trap-jaw ant wields oversize mandibles. Here, she drives a pseudoscorpion from her nest. Sensitive hairs on the jaws detect prey, triggering them to snap shut. Living in tiny colonies of 20 or 30, each ant performs many functions. They "tend to have really specialized anatomies, like these funny jaws that do all sorts of things," says Society grant recipient Mark W. Moffett, who discovered the rare species in Costa Rica. Moffett likes studying small creatures; that way, "you can get a lot done in life."

First she went to the Metro Washington Park Zoo in Portland, Oregon, to observe Asian elephants. "I spent a week sitting at the elephant cage," she said. "And periodically I would feel a throbbing in the air. I had sung in a choir near the pipes of a very big old organ—the lowest pipes. I remember feeling that same feeling.

"I didn't make the connection until I was on the airplane on my way home; then suddenly I realized the elephants might be the source of the throbbing I had felt, if they were making sounds below the range of human hearing."

Later, Payne and her colleagues returned to Portland with recording equipment. "We would make a recording with the tape running very slowly, and then we would speed it up to ten times real speed. That would raise the pitch two and a half octaves. It brought dozens of elephant calls that had been inaudible into our range of hearing."

Payne and her colleagues had found a crucial missing piece in something that had puzzled longtime researchers in African elephant behavior. The re-

KATHARINE B. PAYNE

DES & JEN BARTLETT

Elephants sniff the air in Namibia's Etosha National Park. Katharine Payne (above, with binoculars) and her colleagues record elephant calls. Low-pitched ones may enable widely dispersed elephants to communicate.

searchers had frequently observed elephants raising their ears, as if listening, then freezing for a moment, though no sound was audible to the human ear. They puzzled over sudden synchronous movements of large groups of elephants without any apparent signal. And they wondered (as Payne wrote in NATIONAL GEOGRAPHIC) how male and female elephants find one another to reproduce. Adult males and females live apart, moving over large distances. Breeding males crisscross "large areas in an endless, irritable search for females in breeding season. Well may he feel irritable," Payne said, "for receptive females are a truly scarce resource." Two years of gestation and two years of nursing leave only a few days out of every four years when a female is in estrus. How do the males, moving about independently and sometimes far away, find the estrous female during that short period?

With National Geographic Society support, Payne headed to Amboseli National Park in Kenya to work with Joyce Poole, who had been studying the elephants in the park for many years.

111

A frog-eating bat can avoid devouring a poisonous toad, as Merlin D. Tuttle's experiment proved. The bat backed off at the last second, apparently warned by sensors around its mouth.

There the researchers discovered that African elephants too make infrasound, sound below the range of human hearing. Their calls include the female's special "song," a pattern of deep, resonant rumbles, repeated over half an hour. This call, Poole had observed earlier, usually resulted in the speedy appearance of numerous males.

At Etosha National Park in Namibia, in southwest Africa, Payne and several associates showed that elephants respond to one another's calls over miles. The researchers set up an observation tower and four widely spaced microphones. While one group filmed the elephants' behavior from the tower, another team, in a van, broadcast recordings of elephant rumbles from distant locations. In one instance, researchers in the tower watched two enormous male elephants, Mohammed and Hannibal, at a water hole. "We hear nothing," Payne reported at the time, "but suddenly both elephants lift their heads, stiffen, spread their ears, and hold still. Slowly Mohammed swings his head.... Now Hannibal does the same.... Mohammed has made a decision. He swings around 180 degrees to face southwest, where the van is far out of sight." The two males set off in that direction, ignoring the water and pressing on. "Ten minutes later they pass the van and keep right on moving," much to the relief of the crew within—who had played a recording of the estrous call of an Amboseli female! Clearly the song and the males' response were connected.

But elephants, Payne thinks, may

also have other needs for this sort of long-distance communication: It enables them to keep in touch as they move between water and food in small groups, dispersed over wide areas to avoid overusing fragile environments.

It may well be good—and safe—for an estrous elephant to send her rumbling call across distant valleys. It is a riskier business for an amorous male frog in tropical Panama to sing out his complex *whine-chuck-chuck* call to attract a similarly inclined female.

As Merlin D. Tuttle discovered by chance some years ago, the fringe-lipped bat, *Trachops cirrhosus*, generally dines on those frogs. "Male frogs," he wrote in NATIONAL GEOGRAPHIC, "clearly were faced with a real dilemma! How to attract a mate and not a bat!" He also won-

A clutch of frog-eating bats roosts inside a hollow tree. Grantee Tuttle discovered fine-tuned hearing capabilities that permit the bats to home in on some frog calls to find favored food.

dered how the bat could target a frog of the prey species rather than one of its poisonous cousins. Herpetologists, meanwhile, had their own questions: Why, they had long been asking, did some male frogs seem reluctant to use their longer, more complex mating call, apparently preferred by the females?

Sometimes, to understand the behavior of one animal, you need to study the behavior of another. And so with Society backing, Tuttle, longtime student of bats and founder of Bat Conservation International, teamed up with

BIANCA LAVIES (BOTH)

Rattler Wrangling

Sinuous siblings, 11-day-old timber rattlers twine around their mother (right). Collecting subjects in northern New York State for his study of the species demands a deft touch by William S. Brown (above). Even so, the venomous reptiles have bitten the researcher several times, causing severe discomfort. (The venom rarely brings death to adult humans.) Supported in part by NGS, the Skidmore College professor has censused the reptiles and calculated their growth and survival rate in a long-term study in the wild. He has found that newborns hatched far from their dens use scent to navigate home. The snakes face extinction through shrinking habitat and mindless killing by humans, despite their role in rodent control.

Michael J. Ryan, frog behaviorist from Cornell University. Through field work on Barro Colorado Island, in Panama, they hoped to determine how the bats succeeded in nabbing frogs—and what the frogs did to evade them.

Tuttle and Ryan had theories, but clear answers required clever detective work on bat responses and frog reactions. First of all, they had to figure out whether the bats could discern the specific call of their preferred prey. A captive bat was released into a cage. In opposite corners, speakers emitted calls of either edible frogs or poisonous ones.

"We could hardly contain our excitement when the bat immediately flew to the speaker playing the call of the edible frog. It landed and tried to pry its way through the screen cover of our speaker box." Even after the location of the calls was reversed, the bat made the correct choice.

Somehow over time these New World bats have developed an ability to pick up lower frequencies, in addition to high echolocation frequencies, to home in on the frogs' mating calls.

To test the frogs' reactions, researchers cut out cardboard models that matched the real bats, painted them, and weighted them. These they ran across the frog pond on a fishing line at about normal speed for a frog-eating species as the frogs' calls revved up. "The raucous chorus changed suddenly to total silence," wrote Tuttle. But models of smaller bats, insect-eating varieties, had no such effect. The frogs, it seems, detect

hunting bats visually on all except the darkest nights.

The findings about frogs and bats have implications far beyond the interplay between two neotropical species. Scientists had long surmised, Tuttle said, that "males that made a big display might also incur a much greater risk of being eaten than of getting a mate." These studies are among the first to

demonstrate conclusively that predator activity can directly affect the evolution of courtship communication in prey.

Merlin Tuttle strives to educate people on the role bats play in insect control and pollination and to overcome public fear of the flying mammals he loves.

L. David Mech has similar prejudices to conquer. "There are still too many people in this world who hate

Pups trail Scruffy near an Ellesmere Island cave, where David Mech observed Arctic wolves. They have probably denned here for 700 years.

wolves," the wildlife biologist said. "Most would change their minds if they could share my experience."

His head was freezing in a blustery wind, but Mech didn't care. The wolf he

called Scruffy, the pack's clown, stole away with the wool hat the wind had flipped onto the ground. Mech didn't even mind, on another occasion, seeing his red sleeping bag almost dragged away by a hooligan canid. To live close to a pack of wolves had been Mech's life-long dream. And encounters with the white wolves on Ellesmere Island, in Canada's high Arctic, were intimate indeed. Rock cairns festooned with plastic streamers to scare the animals out of camp only functioned as perfect fire hydrant substitutes.

"It was the highlight of my life," Mech said. Since the late '50s he has studied wolves in the wild—in Michigan, Minnesota, Alaska, and enough other places to be considered the world's leading wolf authority. But never could he get as close to a pack as he did during several summers on Ellesmere, in part supported by NGS research grants.

Mech had known about the wolf packs on Ellesmere for 20 years. "Everywhere else wolves have been so persecuted that they are extremely afraid of humans. One can't get close enough to watch them. But this pack is so remote. They are basically unafraid of humans."

Soon after landing on Ellesmere in 1986 for the first time, Mech searched out the den. Rare in this barren land, it

Pack clown Scruffy totes a treat for himself, a nice fat arctic hare. The yearling male often stayed near the den, serving as baby-sitter for the pups while other adults hunted.

JIM BRANDENBURG (BOTH); ERWIN & PEGGY BAUER (FOLLOWING PAGES)

was a labyrinthine cave, probably used as a den for about 700 years, at the base of a rocky outcropping. At his approach wolves were "running all around me, curious, cautious, alarmed, and upset." He retreated quietly.

Back the next morning, he inched his way up the rise. "I could hardly contain myself," he wrote, "until I peeked over the top….six little beige bundles, along with all seven sprawled-out adults….doing what I later learned they probably do best, or at least most— sleeping. But about an hour later, they awoke, and suddenly all thirteen were running, chasing, playing, and wagging tails. It was a glorious sight!"

The wolves accepted him so completely that upon approaching the den soon afterward, he found a "large furry pile of snoozing pups, the same color as the rocks…but no adults."

In this open terrain he was able to see more. Mech identified individuals and gave them names: Mom, Mid-Back, Lone Wolf, Scruffy, Alpha Male, Left Shoulder, Shaggy. The top-ranking, or alpha, female was not, as had been assumed, always the breeding female. Aloof Mid-Back, a skilled hare hunter, outranked Mom, mother of the pups.

An important thing Mech learned was that "the pack functioned as a kind of finishing school for the pups. They are

Master of his domain, a male guanaco surveys his mountain meadow in Torres del Paine National Park in southern Chile, where William L. Franklin continues long-term studies on this wild camelid species.

leader," acting like tiny pups even though all had participated in the kill.

The wolves apparently posed no threat to Mech, living nearby in his small tent for weeks at a time. He isn't sure why. "I think it has to do with our standing upright," he said.

But for musk-oxen, wolves are killing machines. From the air, Mech had seen wolves hunting many times. Now on Ellesmere he saw a hunt close up for the first time. He was tense as the wolves set the herd of musk-oxen to gyrating. These weren't just any wolves—these were wolves he'd learned to care about. And they could get hurt in the melee, a scene Mech described as "clouds of dust, swerving, twisting, charging; black masses, white streaks, dust—the Stone Age!" In the end the pack brought down three calves and suffered no injuries.

WILLIAM L. FRANKLIN (BOTH)

Franklin's daughter Shelly weighs in one young guanaco at 45 pounds. Scientists view guanacos as wild progenitors of the domestic llama.

under the tutorship of the adults; they learn how to hunt." Feeding was an elaborate ritual. When an adult returns, "pups race each other to the animal, whining and wagging the entire rear halves of their bodies....crouch and wag excitedly, hold their ears back." They fight for food the adult brings. Competition develops aggressiveness.

After a kill, Mech observed, subordinate wolves perform an astonishing submissive ritual. Each was a "fawning mass of insecurity in the face of their

If William L. Franklin were in the high Arctic, he'd probably cheer for the musk-oxen. "Some scientists prefer the predator," Bill Franklin told me. "I'm one who likes the prey." The prey in question is the guanaco, a graceful camelid that once roamed in the millions across the pampas of South America. Franklin's graduate students at Iowa State University, where he teaches animal ecology, like to upset him by calling his subject of choice "puma bait," after its most frequent predator. Financed by the Society, Franklin first headed to South America in 1972, driving in a camper with his wife, two daughters, infant son, and poodle.

In recent years Franklin has settled on a long-term guanaco study site at Torres del Paine National Park, a reserve on the western edge of Patagonia, in the Andean foothills. He learned that male guanacos have a preoccupation with real estate; they stake out territory with dung

Dust bath fluffs a guanaco's wool, increasing insulation. Franklin sees his 20-year study of camelids as a greater contribution "than jumping around from one species to the next."

piles. He also discovered that they expel both their male and female offspring from the natal territory. In what can be a bloody scene, the male bites and kicks, and sometimes takes on a protective mother, to evict a yearling. Such behavior is thought to prevent inbreeding and overgrazing.

"We have really started a new era in these last five or six years, in which we are able to study individual behavior, movements, survivorship, mortality, and parental preference," said Franklin. A more complex social structure is emerging. "We've discovered, for instance, that at birth there are slightly more males than females." Yet by age two or three, six out of ten animals are female. At first researchers thought that the females may have been better nurtured, but there's little difference.

"What's intriguing," Franklin said, "is that in the first year or so one of the major causes of mortality is predation. Why would predators be selecting more males than females? Are males dingbats that don't pay attention to what's going on?" Maybe the females are smarter, or at least more observant.

Franklin has found a low breeding success for males. "Of the 40 percent population that is male, 60 percent live in male groups and 40 percent are territorial. Of the 40 percent that are territorial, only about 40 percent have females." Territorial males await females.

Courtship Rondo

In a pas de deux on a Minnesota
lake, a pair of western grebes perform their characteristic courtship
dance known as "rushing," in
which they seem to run on water.
Backed in part by a 1975 NGS study
grant, ornithologist Gary L.
Nuechterlein became intrigued by
the grebes' spectacular ritual.
Sometimes several males perform
together for a female. No one could
answer why the birds put on such a
high-energy display. After several
years' research, Nuechterlein, now
of North Dakota State University,
thinks the males may be exhibiting
health and vigor to the female. "If
you think of yourself as a female
buying a used car," he says, "and
the set of males as used-car sales-
men, what the female is saying is
'Show me the car. Don't just *tell* me
how great you are!'" Using high-
quality equipment, Nuechterlein
records grebe calls and plays them
back to elicit responses. "If I play a
female call, I can get two males to
do the rush," he says. "Playbacks
almost allow you to talk to the animals—like Dr. Doolittle!" The
racket made by 2,000 birds seemed
like gibberish at first. "But we soon
started realizing that each one of
those individuals is calling to its
own mate and recognizing its mate
among all the calls. When voice-
printed, calls given by a particular
grebe at different times could be
easily matched, as each bird has its
own unique call-frequency pattern.
The more I work on these birds, the
more I appreciate the subtleties of
communication…out there."

Tame peccary gets a cuddle from field biologist George B. Schaller during jaguar studies in Brazil's Mato Grosso.

Right: A rocky ridge shields a shy snow leopard. Such endangered creatures hold tenuously to survival.

The females won't choose a male that doesn't have a piece of real estate, but sometimes, for indecipherable reasons, they ignore one that does.

"Some of these males had established their territory in vegas, or meadows. With luxurious green grass, up to your ankles if not up to your knees, it looked great to me." But the females weren't buying it. Franklin and his colleagues think that these particular meadows are "surrounded by shrubs or steep slopes, favorable for pumas to stalk from, and are therefore more vulnerable to predation. So selection favored those wary females who avoid areas where, even though the food is good, there is a chance of being preyed upon."

As these scientists of animal behavior have carried out their work, many have become aware that their subjects might well not survive into the next century. George Schaller feels that way about many of the animals he has observed. During a career that has spanned four decades, he has probably ranged farther afield than any other of the Society's observers of animal behavior and studied more species. Sometimes—as with his pivotal studies of the Serengeti lions and the giant pandas in China—the Society assisted him only with film. Other times NGS research grants have supported studies on animals as disparate as caimans and capybaras in Brazil's Mato Grosso, and myriad goats and sheep and the snow

leopard of the Himalaya and the Hindu Kush. Aided by a Society grant, Schaller has now headed to northwestern Tibet to help set up a 150,000-square-mile nature reserve in an area not explored by Westerners since 1906.

Schaller first laid eyes on a snow leopard in 1970. She was "peering at me from the spur," he later wrote, "her body so well molded into the contours of the boulders that she seemed a part of them. Her smoky-gray coat...her pale eyes conveyed an image of immense soli-tude.... Then the snow fell more thickly, and dreamlike, the cat slipped away as if she had never been."

Many of Schaller's animals are elusive, and some, like the snow leopard, are slipping closer to extinction.

"I enjoy the science of watching the animals," Schaller told me. "The science is fun. Conservation is not. Conservation is politics, social issues. But you can't morally just do science any more. You've got to worry about the survival of what you are watching."

Adventures in Tracking

By Seymour L. Fishbein

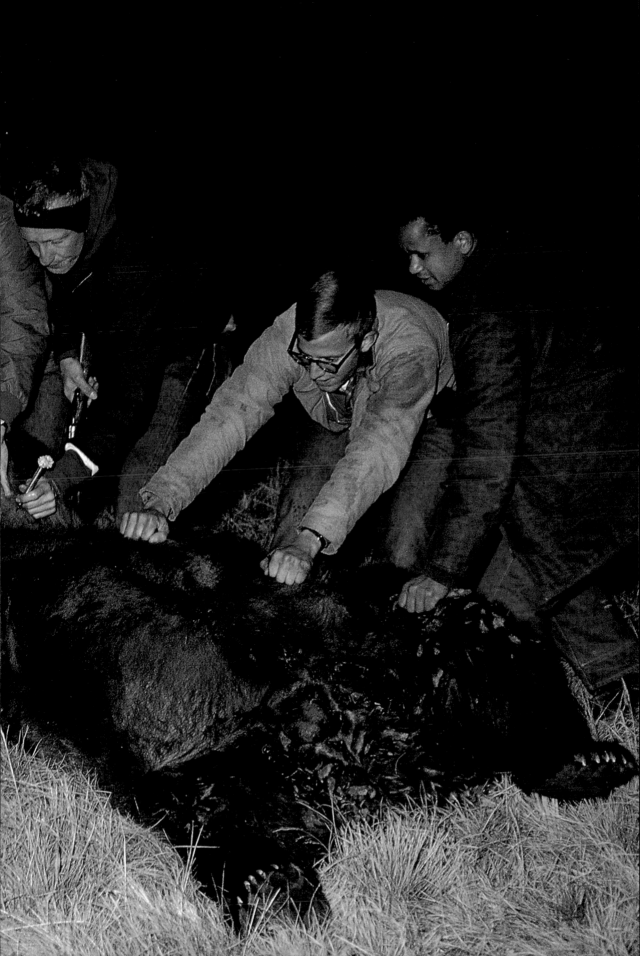

What good is a grizzly? By lantern light in a Yellowstone National Park cabin a generation ago, the bear researchers mulled the question skeptics often threw at them. Then young Karen Craighead spoke up,

FRANK & JOHN CRAIGHEAD (ABOVE AND PRECEDING PAGES)

Drugged grizzly sow, Marian, feels no pain as Yellowstone field aides tattoo an identification number.

Preceding Pages: Craighead team radio collars a grizzly. In 1961, the Craigheads pioneered a tracking tool that soon spread around the world.

"When he's gone, he's gone forever." From that cabin, moved by that simple truth, Karen's father, John, and his twin brother, Frank, ventured across the geyser-strewn wonderland for more than a decade to seek out the haunts and habits of the grizzly bear.

Today, as primeval realms shrink, the list of "gone forever" lengthens by the hour. Edward O. Wilson of Harvard's Museum of Comparative Zoology believes the toll averages three species an hour, 27,000 a year; such a rate, unchecked in the next few decades, could produce a wipeout of life-forms as great as that which extinguished the dinosaurs 65 million years ago.

For some of the animals in this chapter, the knell has come very near—the numbers down to a few score, to less than a dozen, each hatchling, each litter a triumph of science and hope. For others, the trackers' tales are happier. Here is a sampling of nature's still-infinite variety—from the grizzly that may weigh half a ton, to the butterfly that weighs less than two-hundredths of an ounce; from a giant eagle that can crush a monkey, to iridescent mites that siphon nectar; from a haunting bird that hunts underwater, to a secretive rodent that hunts underground.

Untracked terrains of knowledge invite scientific stalkers. Where does the grizzly settle in for the winter? And where the monarch butterfly? How fares the bald eagle in a post-DDT America?

"Science and adventure," in Frank Craighead's words, lured the brothers to wildlife ecology. They found a kindred spirit in the Society, which reported their adventures—and supported their pioneering techniques. These advanced field research from hit-or-miss forays to the space-age marvels of satellites that pinpoint wildlife and map vast wilderness ecosystems.

Fred Urquhart took to the field back in 1916, studying the insects buzzing about near his home. A five-year-old's

A Craighead tracker in Yellowstone aims a loop antenna down canyon. The beep signals it receives can give a bearing on a collared bear as many as 20 miles away.

wonder matured into a lifelong pursuit of the monarch butterfly. In 1993, Fred and Norah—who is wedded to him and to his life's quest—are still at it. Call their home in suburban Toronto, and the tape will answer: "Professor Urquhart speaking. If you are a member of the Insect Migration Association and require more tags, please note the number and spell your last name."

Graduate student Robert Kennedy found his Ph.D. topic the instant he laid eyes on a mounted specimen of an eagle from the Philippines—a gigantic bird of power and presence, yet fading toward oblivion. Its future remains in shadow, but 1992 brought a bright ray: the first Philippine eaglet bred in captivity. It is called Pag-asa—Hope.

For "Black Boots of the Prairies," hope all but died, not once but twice. A century ago the black-footed ferret, perhaps a million strong, enjoyed room and board in prairie dog towns from Mexico to Canada. In recent decades it vanished, popped up again, then dwindled until not a single wild ferret was known. Conservation biologist Tim Clark and federal and state wildlife officials rode the roller coaster; unbeknownst to them, a fecund ménage à trois—an adult male and two females—had survived, the seed stock of hope.

By 1959, when the Craigheads began their Yellowstone study, the most powerful carnivore on the continent had been rapidly disappearing from the lower 48. Field science had entered a much more complex age, seeking a mountain of detail about diet, ranges, and life cycles.

"We had to be able to recognize individuals," observes John, "measure them, record family histories. We wanted to know at what age and how often females breed and how many cubs are produced. Essentially this is the kind of information the Census Bureau gets on human populations, except all they need is the questionnaire. We had to figure how to capture and handle an aggressive animal, largely nocturnal, that wintered in a den. It wasn't easy."

The two Craigheads lured grizzlies into traps and shot them with syringe darts loaded with a muscle relaxant or tranquilizer to immobilize them. "Because we tended to underdose…thus erring in favor of the bear," wrote Frank in his book *Track of the Grizzly*, "an untimely return to consciousness was not unheard of." Ivan the Terrible, for example: Unable to hold the struggling giant, the crew raced for a station wagon. They barely made it; Ivan swiped at the vehicle as it roared away.

Each trapped grizzly was marked with identification—metal ear tags, tattoos on lip or armpit, and colored plastic streamers. Much was learned, and much

remained unknown. Backcountry sightings often depended on chance. "So we struck on the idea," John recalls, "of putting a radio on the bear."

Two years' work with electronics experts produced a lightweight transmitter housed in a bear collar, a directional receiver, and antennnas. Then, one fall day in 1961, in the wildlife paradise of Hayden Valley, a new sound was joined to the honking of geese and

the bugling of bull elk. A hand-held receiver picked up the high-pitched beeps that originated from the collar of the first grizzly to be tracked by radio.

John Craighead remembers the scoffing: "'Just a gimmick, never gonna be much use.' It's probably one of the most useful techniques ever developed to study wild animals. The National Geographic Society was the first to put up funding. This enabled us to develop,

Fishing grizzly joins a salmon run in Alaska. With Society aid, the Craigheads took biotelemetry into the space age—researching remote ecosystems by satellite.

test, and apply the technology; after that it was much easier to get support."

For years the Craigheads tried in vain to track grizzlies to their winter dens. In 1963, radiotelemetry did it.

John Craighead dodges a possible charge by a drug-dazed Yellowstone grizzly. Researchers took care with dosages. Too much could kill a bear; too little risked human life or limb.

Frank and two assistants followed a sow through fresh snow. "The woods were silent except for the signal," wrote Frank. "The deep wing beats of a great gray owl we flushed made no sound." Atop some fallen timber, Frank heard a beeping of constant strength from all directions. Was the bear directly underneath?

One of the assistants, Maurice Hornocker, thought it might be; he braced himself on the slippery logs so that he could swing his gun, if need be— the tracker's defense of last resort, but never resorted to. "There it is!" whispered Maurice. He pointed to litter on packed snow in front of a cave. "Wonder if she has her yearlings with her," he mused. "We can't take a chance on riling her now," Frank replied. No one disagreed. The lowest limbs on the nearby lodgepoles were 30 feet from the ground.

In the late 1960s, the Craigheads embraced satellite technology to monitor the radio signals. The orbiting vehicle receives location data on every pass, and the biologist can track from computer readouts. John Craighead also set in motion a long-range project of joining Landsat imagery, ground surveys, and computer analysis to map the varieties of plant life across broad wilderness tracts. Such knowledge can help preserve intact wilderness ecosystems.

Now in their late 70s, the brothers still keep track of the grizzly's fortunes. In Yellowstone, notes John, "we found that the grizzly bear reproduced very slowly, and that if anything cataclysmic happened to a population, it would take a long time to recover."

A few decades ago park officials, hoping to restore more natural conditions, decided to close garbage dumps where grizzlies had been feeding for most of a century. The Craigheads warned that an abrupt closing would send the bears foraging through campgrounds, with hazard to visitors and, ultimately, destruction of bears.

The dumps were closed. The Craigheads left Yellowstone, their protests stirring a national controversy. The bears wandered, discovered fatal attractions, and were lost in unprecedented numbers. In 1975 the grizzly was listed as threatened south of Canada under the Endangered Species Act.

Dick Knight, leader of the Interagency Grizzly Bear Study Team, estimated the population in late 1992 to be at least 250, trending slowly upward. The Craigheads' work, Knight says, "was a landmark. If they hadn't had the data and hadn't raised hell when the park closed the dumps, and if we didn't get another study going that showed the grizzlies declining, we would have had a tough situation today...."

Some 40 years ago Judith McIntyre,

Brown Bear Society

Gentle demeanor of an Alaskan brown bear sow nuzzling her cub belies the ferocity with which she will defend it. Early research on this larger, coast-dwelling cousin of the grizzly focused on competition among the bears as they gathered to feast on spawning salmon.

More recently, in a Society-backed study on Admiralty Island, Robert and Johanna Fagen have discovered surprising playfulness, even among adult brown bears long considered "antisocial, and down-right cranky." The Fagens credit such revelations with changing public attitudes about the bears—thus helping to protect them.

Its bill low, a common loon rears up to defend its nest. Judith McIntyre studied lonely haunts of the northern diver, its eerie nocturnal music, and the perils it faces.

MICHAEL S. QUINTON (BOTH)

a French major and prospective interior decorator, attended a Craighead seminar at Carleton College in Minnesota. "In four years," she laughs, "I heard dozens of seminars, but that was the only one I remembered. Wildlife. Wow! I forgot the exact words, but I never forgot the enthusiasm they generated."

Then there was foreign study, and then decorating Minneapolis interiors. "I was a typical 1950s dilettante," she says. "I was interested in birds so I took a course in ornithology." At 40 she thought a Ph.D. in zoology would be nice. "An adviser said, 'Why don't you

work on loons? There's a lot to be done. C'mon, let's get into a canoe and go look at some.' And so we did. And I said, 'I'll do it.' Twenty-five years later, I'm still doing it," declares Judith McIntyre, professor of biology at Utica College of Syracuse University.

She has seen the common loons wing in from coastal winter retreats to northern nesting grounds "as newly thawed lakes sparkle under an April sun." She covered the water wars over territorial battlefields, loon against loon, and even witnessed a kill—"a female attacking an intruder until the stranger

Its bill high, a loon in handsome breeding plumage signals with nonaggressive wing flapping. Loons shake their wings and stretch as they shed water and preen their feathers.

loon was bloodied and dove into the depths of the lake, never to be seen again." She has watched them build nests and sit on the eggs—"hot sun beating on their backs, blackflies biting their heads, summer storms spilling rain and hail on them," until "around the longest day of the year, loon pairs become loon families." She offered them artificial islands for nesting, away from disturbance, and has known the pleasure of seeing those offerings accepted.

Dr. McIntyre became a connoisseur and interpreter of what one observer called "the most thrilling...of all the voices of the northern wilderness." The voice of the loon is the voice of wild places far from human haunts. Yet the calls, as Henry David Thoreau noted, sound "singularly human." Weirdly human, too easily associated with "loony," which in bygone days referred to a poor soul driven daft by changes in Luna, the moon.

The bird's repertoire, far from loony, represents rather a sane way of communicating. Short hooting calls establish and maintain contact between loons. Wailing sounds, writes Judith McIntyre in *The Common Loon: Spirit of Northern*

MICHAEL S. QUINTON (BOTH)

With baton microphone and tape recorder, McIntyre (above) captured the spectacular loon calls and delved into their meaning. In courtship, loons prefer a quiet ritual (right)—tandem swimming, head turning, bill dipping.

Lakes, "seems to be the loon version of 'come here' or 'here I come.'" Tremolos sound alarms, and yodeling is the male territorial song.

Dr. McIntyre deciphered some of the messages at a large lake in northern Saskatchewan, a thriving loon community of 86 pairs. Supported by a pilot grant from National Geographic, she and her graduate student played loon calls to the territorial pairs all through the breeding season and observed the responses. One midnight in August lingers in memory: "Sheets of northern lights were playing all over the sky, curtains rippling up, down, across. Dozens and dozens of loon voices came from every direction. Most nights the calls might die down for about 20 minutes. Now they'd pause for a few seconds, and erupt again just like the lights. Marvelous." Yodeling, quavering tremolos, piercing wails—the orchestration of a primal nocturne.

"Can the magic of our northern wilderness last when we make ourselves part of it?" asks Judith McIntyre. Yes, she insists: "With time and care, humans and loons can fish the same lakes, children and loon chicks can swim the same

138

FOLLOWING PAGES: TOM & PAT LEESON

waters." The dilettante has become "the Loon Lady," who helped reverse a century and more of retreat by the common loon. A newspaper column about her work brought a thousand responses and led to Minnesota's Project Loon Watch in 1971. Loon lovers set up similar projects across the nation and north into Canada. But even where a human welcome is assured, there remain the hazards of heavy metal pollution, acid precipitation, toxic lead fishing sinkers, atmospheric contaminants, and organic pollutants. The loon fishes in troubled waters.

Those of us who despise dams as despoilers of nature must swallow hard the positive news from Judith McIntyre and her graduate school colleague, Thomas Dunstan: Loons find nesting habitat at *(Continued on page 144)*

A helpless newborn gets a helping of meat in Alaska, where bald eagles are plentiful. In the Midwest, Tom Dunstan radiotracked fledglings and saw new hope for our magnificent national bird.

Avian Success Story

With claws extended, an osprey (above) swoops down to snatch a fish. Commonly called the fish hawk, this bird of prey marks a wildlife success story. Once widespread around the world, ospreys, for reasons then unknown, began to decline in the 1950s. Roger Tory Peterson and other ornithologists noticed the population plummeting. A flourishing colony of 150 active nests within a ten-mile radius of Peterson's home in Old Lyme, Connecticut, was suddenly failing to produce young. Was the problem raccoons or egg collectors? With Society support—a small grant in 1962 to erect 21 secure nesting plat-

forms in his area—Peterson hoped to reverse the trend. "But production of young remained…scarcely 13 percent of the norm," he wrote. The problem was more complex than predation. The widely used pesticide DDT, researchers eventually discovered, accumulated in fish the ospreys ate and in their eggs. Painstaking detective work by many scientists was needed to show a direct link between the toxic chemicals and the breeding failures. In 1969 and 1970, backed by Geographic grants, James R. Koplin documented the decline of ospreys around Montana's Flathead Lake. He confirmed that even after the region stopped spraying with DDT, the lake's waters remained contaminated.

Koplin found DDT residues and dead embryos in the eggs, and flaking and cracked shells. He concluded that the Flathead Lake ospreys' difficulties in reproducing were related to DDT contamination.

In the early 1970s, after many studies, laws banned almost all uses of DDT. Soon came the ultimate proof of the theory: a remarkable recovery of populations of ospreys and other birds of prey.

the impoundments behind dams. Dunstan studies bald eagles that fish the wintry roils below the 26 Mississippi River locks and dams "between the Saints"—St. Paul and St. Louis.

Near one of these, Tom Dunstan found habitat that was ideal for an eagle researcher. He is currently professor of biology at Western Illinois University in Macomb; 45 miles west, hundreds of eagles fish for gizzard shad below Lock and Dam 19 and roost nearby in the Cedar Glen Eagle Roost. Professor and students observe them there; and in the springtime, when classes let out and northern Minnesota lakes thaw, Dunstan, like the eagles, makes the seasonal commute to the country where he grew up, ever in admiration of the soaring white-headed birds.

"This is the national bird, and it was my long-term goal to study it and protect it. I've lived that dream," he says. He has followed the eagles year-round since the perilous early '60s, spurred on by a Society grant in 1971. The bald eagle had been victimized by habitat loss, poaching, purposeful killing, and contamination of its food. In 1972, an aroused nation banned the pesticide DDT, which had concentrated in fish and was then ingested by fish-eating birds. Not only birds. "I have lived on the summer breeding grounds in the Chippewa National Forest," Dunstan says. "I discovered that bald eagles were eating the same thing that my Finnish and Swedish relatives ate and risked the same chemical problems."

In the Chippewa, he reported in

NATIONAL GEOGRAPHIC, he has watched the eagles "building their nests, feeding their young, fussing at the nestlings' first flights, drifting on broad wings through summer skies." Miniature transmitters attached to nestbound eaglets enabled researchers to track the juveniles when they left the breeding sites. As autumn glazed the lakes and set the aspens, oaks, and maples ablaze, the "eagle tracks" led south.

The national forest counted 6 successful eagle nests in 1963; they produced 10 young. By 1992 observers had spotted activity at 175 nests, 101 of them bringing forth 141 eaglets. "Definitely uphill, though the breeding population may be peaking," concludes Dunstan. The Chippewa, with 1,200 lakes and 155 named streams, may be reaching its carrying capacity.

In the frigid valley between the

Talons clenched on a dead snake, a Philippine eaglet hones its skills. Losing habitat, as documented by grantee Bob Kennedy, the species nears oblivion amid efforts to save it.

Saints, bald eagles find a warm welcome. Conservation groups and government resource agencies have joined forces to set aside protected winter roosts. In towns along the river, Bald

Radio-tagged and released, a young Philippine eagle flies off to freedom. With funding from the Society, Bob Kennedy studies the birds in terrain wracked by civil unrest and poverty.

Eagle Days attract thousands of people. Often Tom Dunstan is there, with live birds of prey, never failing to remind folks "that no mechanical instrument can sample environmental pollutants and tell us more about environmental quality than these raptorial birds. They and we sit highest in the food chain. When they're in trouble, we're in trouble." And there's no end to trouble: Though DDT impact in the U. S. may be gone, mercury, lead, and PCBs endure.

Even so, counting the aggregations in Canada and Alaska, the bald eagle numbers in the tens of thousands. The Philippine eagle, bigger and fiercer, numbers perhaps 100 or 200. That's including the "maybes," hidden deep in the tropical rain forest. Dennis Salvador, executive director of the Philippine Eagle Conservation Program Foundation, knew of only 50 birds in the summer of 1992. The species "is rapidly slipping from endangerment to extinction," he reported.

It was known as the monkey-eating eagle when Bob Kennedy saw it as a stuffed bird. Drawn to the image of power and the species' well-known plight, he met it on the wing not long after as a Peace Corps volunteer in Mindanao. At home some years later, the newly fledged Ph.D. in ornithology found his first postgraduate job in the field of interior decorating. "To get money to go back, I painted houses in Chicago for $12 an hour—a salary that I have only recently surpassed," says Dr. Kennedy, a deputy director of the Cincinnati Museum of Natural History.

He and some colleagues—a trio of conservation-minded filmmakers— saved enough from house painting to start a laborious documentation of the vanishing raptor. Soon came the first of three Geographic grants. Nests were hard to find and hard to reach at heights of more than a hundred feet. Once, wrote Kennedy, he "dangled slothlike by hands and feet," inching along a rope to a nest. As he examined the nestling in it, the mother swooped down, scratching him with the great talons that capture and kill flying lemurs, monkeys, hawks, bats, cobras, even small deer.

Surprisingly, one pair nested amid sparse forest cover. "The belief had been that the eagles required virgin forest or advanced second growth," observed Kennedy. "Apparently, the birds can adapt to man's presence if enough forest survives, and assuming, of course, they

Giant tortoises in Isabela's Volcan Alcedo

Galápagos Tortoises

Keeping cool, giant tortoises wallow in a pond on Isabela, largest of the Galápagos Islands. Though only 11 survive, 14 separate sub-species of the tortoise evolved in the archipelago off the west coast of South America, offering intriguing insights to Charles Darwin in formulating his theory of evolution.

Slaughtered by early mariners and affected by introduced animals, the tortoise population has plunged from an estimated quarter million to perhaps 15,000. Some 40 National Geographic research grants have backed studies in the Galápagos, particularly on ways to protect various rare island species.

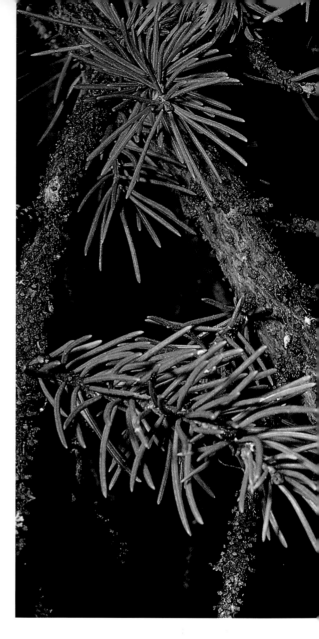

are not shot or captured." A captive breeding program was initiated in 1977. For 15 years all efforts failed, until the eagle named Pag-asa pipped its shell.

By the mid-1980s the program had switched emphasis from eagle management to people management, to encourage selective cutting and discourage poaching and slashing and burning. Some 17 million people in the region, says Dennis Salvador, are "considered to

Broad-tailed hummingbird and her nearly grown chick (right) face frosty mountain nights and a fight for nectar with the feisty rufous hummingbird (above). William Calder conducts long-term studies of both species.

be the country's poorest of the poor." With international support, Salvador's foundation has offered incentives to help the forest people improve their lot without harming the environment. There's not much time. In the 1970s, Bob Kennedy thought as many as 500 Philip-

pine eagles survived; now, at most, 200. Amid the gloom shines Hope, Pag-asa.

Whatever the future holds for the avian giants, it does not seem to weigh heavily on the radiant lilliputians that Bill Calder tracks. He has followed them from winter homes in Mexico's Western Sierra Madre to coastal Alaska, where the rufous hummingbird breeds, to the Colorado Rockies, where the broad-tailed hummingbird nests. Here, any chill night can cause an energy crisis for a bird that weighs a ninth of an ounce.

"What does it mean to be small?"

reflects Professor Calder of the University of Arizona. "Here is a bird that makes its heat with no more flesh on its body than my little finger has. When the temperature gets down to freezing, my finger gets numb, but that little bird is still sitting on the nest warming eggs."

Calder has been prying into secrets of minimalist strategies for more than 20 years, with extended support from the National Geographic Society. At the Rocky Mountain Biological Laboratory in Gothic, Colorado, he found that when broad-tail hens fail to store enough fuel for a cold night, they conserve energy by lowering body temperatures and slipping into short-term hibernation. Before sunrise, an internal clock turns up the furnace so they fly out to refuel from wildflower nectars or from artificial feeders, where observers trap, band, color-mark, and study the birds.

Females that are still nesting in July compete for food with an invasion of rufous hummingbirds on their southbound return to Mexico. The feisty, brilliantly garbed rufous hummingbird is an exceptional traveler, outperforming, elderly female, at least 12 years old, had returned to Gothic enough summers, reported Calder, "to have become a great-great-great-great-great-great-great-great-great-grandmother!"

Males do not live as long. Many seem to burn out after a single arduous breeding season—but, oh, what a season! Early birds claim territories and fiercely defend them, with rose-red gorgets flashing and a trill whistling from their wingtips.

During a 15-hour day, they often resist the floral sweets to stay in fighting and courting trim. Around a feeder one male averaged 41 chases and 43 climbing, diving courtship displays per hour. He fended off rival males; how he fared with the females remained hidden from the eyes of science by willow brush. At dusk the males increase their weight by as much as 40 percent during a feeding orgy, sustenance for the night fast and another lean, mean, and ardent day.

As if these animated rubies and emeralds were not gift enough in their sparkling presence, they perform an additional service on burned or cut-over land. As new growth blooms, hummingbirds visit the flowers, drawing nectars and bearing pollens—hastening the regeneration of life and beauty.

Each autumn an orange glow coats the somber green of pine and eucalyptus trees on California's storied Monterey Peninsula. Thousands of tourists converge to see the western monarch butterflies come home for the winter. Where, wondered Fred Urquhart, did the great hordes of eastern monarchs find winter refuge? And how to track them?

After years of experimenting, Dr. Urquhart discovered a suitable marker —an adhesive tag like those used to stick the price on glassware. A numbered tag bearing a return address was folded over a wing, and the monarch flew off. Hundreds of thousands were tagged by

PAUL A. ZAHL; KENNETH BRUGGER (OPPOSITE)

Sierra Madre skies swirl with eastern monarch butterflies—the winter haven Fred Urquhart sought for years. With wings shut, western monarchs (above) resemble dead leaves.

by one measure, the arctic tern, distance champion of the bird world. In a single migration, notes Calder, the tern may fly 10,900 miles, or 46 million times its body length; the tiny hummingbird flies 49 million body lengths in the 2,700 miles from Mexico to Alaska.

Should the invaders win the food fight, the broad-tail, rather than starve, abandons her nest. But a generous life span may enable her to try again. One

volunteers. Recaptured specimens—including one that had flown 2,050 miles—were returned to Urquhart. One day in 1975, Ken and Cathy Brugger, volunteers residing in Mexico, reported exciting news. Before long, the Bruggers and Fred and Norah Urquhart labored up the slopes of a 10,000-foot mountain in the Sierra Madre. There, in a forested valley, ended a quest that had haunted Fred Urquhart for nearly half a century.

"Butterflies—millions upon millions of monarch butterflies!" he wrote in NATIONAL GEOGRAPHIC. "They clung in tightly packed masses to every branch and trunk of the tall, gray-green *oyamel* trees…. Breathless from the altitude, my legs trembling from the climb, I muttered aloud, 'Unbelievable!'"

Around the time Fred Urquhart exulted in the sight of those millions, the known number of black-footed ferrets, another wide-ranging North American native, stood at zero. It stood that way

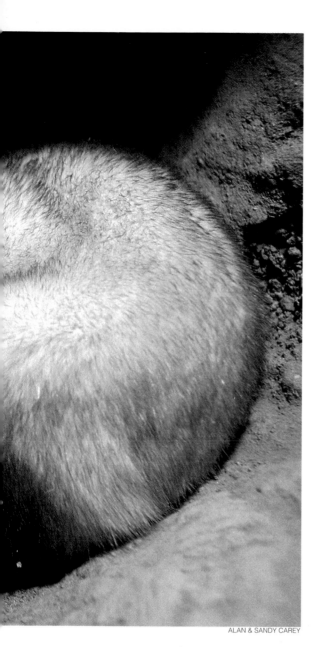

ALAN & SANDY CAREY

Once so rare that $10,000 was offered for a proven find, the black-footed ferret bred well in captivity and has begun a return to natural lairs.

for the rest of the decade. The masked little raider preyed on the prairie dog, long regarded as a despoiler of cropland and range; a killing spree that lasted most of this century had wiped out millions of prairie dogs. As the prairie dog went, so went the predator. Now the fer-

ret seemed to have joined the passenger pigeon and the great auk.

For eight years, with the help of National Geographic and many conservation groups, conservation biologist Tim Clark searched for ferrets, spreading an appeal throughout prairie dog country. In the fall of 1981, John Hogg's ranch dog killed a strange "mink" near Meeteetse, Wyoming. When Hogg tried to have it mounted, taxidermist Larry LaFranchi recognized the rare find and spread the word. The Hoggs and government officials invited Dr. Clark to join the intense conservation effort.

Researchers stood vigil around the Meeteetse prairie dog colonies, spotlights probing for telltale green eyeshine. They followed radio signals and footprints in the snow. In all they counted about 300 individuals—ferrets at play, ferrets leading litters, ferrets ferreting out prairie dogs. Suddenly, in 1985, came a catastrophic decline, attributed to canine distemper. The last wild ferrets were taken captive—a total of 18, including adults and many young. Finally, captive breeding took hold, and 1992 and 1993 were banner years.

"The captives produced a bumper crop, and we have about 300 now," reported Dr. Clark. "And 49 were reintroduced to the wild near Medicine Bow, Wyoming. They produced six young— the first ferrets born in the wild since 1986." All from that founding remnant. "Yes. If it hadn't been for that male and those two breeding females back in 1986," muses Tim Clark, "we'd have been out of the ferret business."

If—. There's a secret that needs unlocking. In that dark sanctuary, where the choice was life, or gone forever.

Exploring
Beneath the Sea

By Richard M. Crum

All hands were busy. Scientists at the Woods Hole Oceanographic Institution in Massachusetts were clearing the decks for a return trip to the site on the Pacific floor where, in 1977, they had helped make a sensational discovery.

Slated to join this 1979 expedition was Emory Kristof, a NATIONAL GEOGRAPHIC staffer specializing in deep-sea

Mysterious "dandelion" of the deep, photographed by the first underwater solid-state camera, turns out to be a new kind of siphonophore.

photography. He outlined the expedition's promise: "The discovery of deep-sea-life communities in the hot water vents of the Galápagos Rift...offered an unexpected bonus....The biological questions raised...are enough to send the whole science of marine biology off into new, unexplored directions."

Kristof proposed to bring back the first deep-sea images taken with a revolutionary new device: a tubeless, color video TV camera. If successful, this

charge-coupled device (CCD) would give Woods Hole a major data-gathering tool as a permanent facility on *Alvin*, the institution's renowned submersible.

Oceanographers prize cameras for research. Candid photographs show ocean creatures in their habitats, unimpaired by the changes in pressure and temperature that occur when they are hauled to the surface for study. The CCD camera offered even more. It could produce images suitable for processing as still photographs for the Society's magazine and as film for a TV documentary.

Huge costs and risks were involved. Few ventures other than space probes require more high-tech instruments and life-support systems than oceanographic missions. Modern ships include sleek submersibles equipped with mechanical arms and microelectronic eyes; deployment can cost as much as $25,000 a day.

For years, grants from the National Geographic Society have helped defray such costs, especially in the area of underwater photography. It was Grant No. 1928 for the CCD camera that excited Kristof. "There never has been a network show on deep ocean work...," he noted in his 1979 memo. The Geographic had, however, underwritten many scientific firsts in underwater imaging, including in 1927 the world's first published underwater natural-color

Newly discovered creatures of the abyss, bloodred tube worms house bacteria that break down hydrogen sulfide to make food for their hosts.

Preceding Pages: Weightless in a medium 800 times heavier than air, a diver collects specimens in the world's least explored realm—the sea.

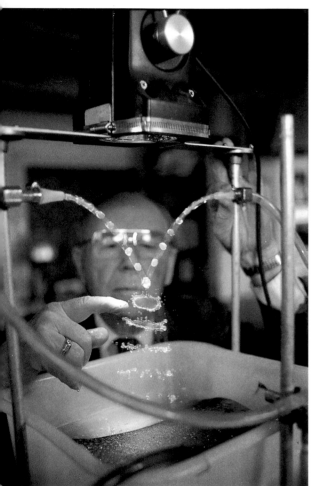

Papa Flash: Harold Edgerton casts a strobe light on flowing water to reveal individual drops. His high-speed flash allowed a new look at ocean secrets.

photographs of marine life. By synchronizing a brass-encased camera and explosive flashlight powder, ichthyologist W. H. Longley produced spectacular Autochromes of reef fishes off the Florida Keys.

The Society offered mainly technical

services during its early association with undersea exploration, but official grants soon followed. Few have proved more significant than the 1934 grant awarded to naturalist William Beebe.

Beebe and engineer Otis Barton put to sea off Bermuda in the world's first deep oceanographic research submersible, the bathysphere. This small tethered chamber penetrated inky coldness half a mile down. "The only other place comparable to these...nether regions," Beebe noted, "must surely be naked space...where sunlight has no grip."

Beebe and Barton were the first humans to come face-to-face with alien creatures of the abyss and live to tell about it. Of one dive Beebe wrote: "I saw some creature...dart toward the window, turn sideways and—explode! ...The flash...illumined my face...I saw a large red shrimp and an outpouring fluid of flame."

Nearly two decades later, Beebe's boldness infused the National Geographic Society-*Calypso* Marine Archeological Expedition. "It is one of the most comprehensive oceanographic expeditions of modern times, a scientific party that plans to spend the next four years in undersea explorations...around the globe," Society President Gilbert H. Grosvenor announced in 1952.

The expedition's leader was Frenchman Jacques-Yves Cousteau, co-inventor of the Aqua-Lung and captain of the research ship *Calypso*. Cousteau brought the age of television to undersea archaeology. Off the French Mediterranean coast, he linked a submarine camera to shipboard monitors; the telecast allowed archaeologists to follow *Calypso* divers as they excavated the world's oldest known cargo ship. Up from the sunken Greco-Roman argosy came samples of its 2,200-year-old freight, jugs of wine, and fine Campanian pottery.

In the Mediterranean Sea, *Calypso*

deployed sonar and camera to upgrade precision mapping of the seabed, and in the Persian Gulf the ship logged the first comprehensive offshore oil survey by divers. The Society-*Calypso* voyages proved Aqua-Lung diving and photography valuable as marine research tools.

Working off *Calypso* was Luis Marden, a GEOGRAPHIC staffer and one of the first professional photographers to take a camera beneath the sea. He particularly remembers anchoring at Assumption Island in 1955. Fanned by the trade winds, this remote paradise forms part of the Aldabra Island group in the Indian Ocean. "All my diving had been on coral reefs," Marden said. "Yet I had never seen so magnificent a sight."

He hefted an Aqua-Lung onto his back. Then, with a twin-flash Leica in waterproof housing in his hand, he dropped backward into the bay. "The luminous transparency of the warm water bathed me in light." Rainbow-colored fish clustered in innocent curiosity. "I tried to take close-ups of the fish," Marden said, "but they came too near to stay in focus. When I backed off, they came with me."

One large grouper followed Marden everywhere. Nicknamed "Ulysses," the 60-pound fish liked to poke the camera lens with its blunt head.

As if preening for a screen test, Ulysses pestered Cousteau's moviemakers, who were shooting a feature film, *The Silent World*. Ulysses blundered into setups so often that the "lens louse" had to be kept in a holding cage during filming. Still, the gutsy bottom-dweller stole major scenes.

Ulysses became the Aldabras' first movie star when *The Silent World* premiered a year later. The Academy Award-winning film and Marden's series of published color photographs heightened public enthusiasm for Aqua-Lung diving and undersea photography.

LUIS MARDEN

Aqua-Lung frees a diver to explore as deep as 300 feet. In the 1950s, Society grants helped diving and underwater photography become valuable tools.

In the shadow of this popularity stood "Papa Flash."

Harold Edgerton, a professor at the Massachusetts Institute of Technology, was crowned Papa Flash after developing the stroboscope. This high-speed electronic flash fires brighter-than-sun

THOMAS J. ABERCROMBIE, NGS STAFF

exposures as brief as a millionth of a second, stopping fast action.

Early in 1951, Edgerton welcomed editorial help from Luis Marden on a manuscript about hummingbirds for NATIONAL GEOGRAPHIC. A Society grant had allowed the inventor to field-test new lightweight strobe equipment, which froze the flight of the birds in their first color close-ups. Later, Edgerton remarked to Marden that he had always wanted to make an automatic camera that would flash underwater.

Marden sent a memo to the Geographic's Committee for Research and Exploration, which approved funding for Edgerton to build his underwater flash camera. The Society also introduced Papa Flash to Cousteau. By 1953, Edgerton's underwater strobe photos were enlightening marine scientists.

Biologists had never before viewed the starfish in its true habitat. They thought that this echinoderm lay flat on the seafloor, as it did when it was laid out on deck. But an Edgerton series on a slender-armed brittle star showed it thrashing about like a demented octopus, snatching food from the currents.

In 1956, a Society grant set up the first photographs of the 25,354-foot-deep Romanche Trench, then thought to be the Atlantic Ocean's lowest point. Edgerton's first strobe image, Cousteau

recalled, showed "...tiny pale fish shapes...," proving "that mobile species lived nearly two miles deeper than had been previously observed...."

Eager to bring a lens to bear on the elusive deep dwellers, Cousteau and Edgerton improvised an ingenious device, the towed camera sled. They built it from a converted metal diving ladder. The ladder's upcurved handrails made excellent runners. Straps fastened the camera and flash tubes to the rungs. A plank inserted crosswise served as a hydrofoil. Tied to a cable, the National Geographic flag appended to its side, the rig sank into the dusky Tyrrhenian Sea—to its demise, the crew thought.

Starfish House descends to a reef in the Red Sea. For a month in 1963 this chamber sheltered a crew of five, who demonstrated that humans could live and work in a subsea colony.

Instead, the sled tracked steadily for three miles, clicking the first continuous strip picture of the seafloor. Oceanographers quickly adopted the camera sled as a standard tool.

The best underwater camera flying blind was a poor substitute for direct observation by human eyes, however. "We needed a radically new submarine, something small, agile," Cousteau said.

In 1959, the Society backed French

R and D money are used in work leading up to a grant," Kristof explained. "The Geographic supplied all the 35mm color film for ANGUS at Galápagos in 1977, as well as shipboard processing."

The Galápagos Rift is a boundary between separating plates of oceanic crust in the Pacific Ocean. Along the seam magma wells up, cools, and cracks. Cold seawater seeps into the fissures, and intense heat and pressure cause the percolating water to leach minerals from the surrounding rocks. Forced back up to the seafloor by convection, the water emerges in warm streams or in scalding geysers. Scientists had speculated about hydrothermal vents, but they never saw an active one, until 1977.

ROBERT GOODMAN

Oceanaut Jacques Cousteau (center) and wife Simone visit Starfish House. Aided by Society grants, he built the four-armed headquarters of his undersea village called Conshelf Two.

and American engineers in turning a Cousteau idea into a two-man diving saucer. They christened it *Denise*. Hydrojet nozzles propelled the rudderless craft. Sea trials proved that *Denise*, the world's first jet submarine, could bank and scoot underwater like a fish.

A submersible and a towed camera sled work well together. The sled scouts targets, and the submersible takes scientists down for a firsthand look. The most successful sled-submersible team consists of ANGUS and *Alvin*, operated by Woods Hole.

Both devices have benefited from National Geographic aid. "A lot of the Geographic's technical services and

On a midnight flight in February, ANGUS clicked off 13 photographs of unusual white clam shells around a Galápagos vent. White dots also speckled the photos. Probably chemical splotches on the negatives, a scientist said. But a few of the scientists wondered why the spots cast a shadow.

Woods Hole scientist Robert Ballard went down in *Alvin* to inspect the seabed. "Coming out of small cracks... was warm, shimmering water that quickly turned a cloudy blue as manganese and other chemicals...were deposited on the lava surface," he noted.

"But even more interesting was the presence of a dense biological community living in and around the active vents. The animals were large, particularly the white clams...." Certain species defied explanation, especially by a geologist. Expedition members had prepared themselves to deal with the seabed's chemical and physical structure. Instead they were gaping at strange seafloor life-forms more than 8,000 feet below the surface— and no biologist was aboard to help explain the creatures.

The geologists collected a living specimen, preserved it as best they could in the only bottle of formaldehyde aboard, and returned to Woods Hole. Evidence of ample life from a zone long thought to be too cold, too pressured, and too dark for much life astounded the scientific world. A second Galápagos expedition was quickly planned. This time the crew would include marine biologists to appraise the life-forms.

Alvin was made ready. Originally a lefty, the submersible got a second mechanical arm—a right one—to hold the CCD camera. Ballard petitioned the Society's Committee for Research and Exploration to fund the radically new imaging package: "The television camera will be closer to the various subject matters in the vent areas than any other camera system. With [it] mounted on its own pan and tilt unit, we will be able to take high-quality color, close-up pictures of the smaller organisms, which are difficult to capture and later identify."

Alvin flexed its new camera arm during 20 dives to the Galápagos vents early in 1979. Hot mineral springs teemed with microbes able to convert toxic hydrogen sulfide into food energy. Living off the bacteria were larger organisms: outsize clams, brown mussels, ghostly white crabs.

DAVIS MELTZER

Cutaway look at Starfish House: One arm contains galley, toilet, and lab. A sharkproof grille guards the diver's entrance. Two arms hold bunks. The central chamber houses control center, crew, and a parrot on duty to detect any dangerous gas leak.

Here in a submerged realm of eternal night was a food chain flourishing on chemicals instead of sunshine. The process, known as chemosynthesis, made the biologists blink. The belief that sunlight is always the main source of life-giving energy was dead wrong.

Thriving near some of the hot springs were waving forests of red-tipped tube worms. In one area, *Alvin*'s new camera eyes spied 12-foot tube worms, the tallest ever seen. Some of the vent creatures fit known niches. The white dots that had prompted questions earlier were not splotches on film but rarely seen *(Continued on page 168)*

Virtuosos of the Sea

As bulky as a touring bus and as graceful as an acrobat, a humpback whale (above) breaches with explosive leaps above the waves.

The 40-ton, 45-foot-long humpback chirps and yodels wild melodies, "made of sequences of sounds which are repeated to form long and complex themes," explains zoologist Roger Payne. "A song can have two to eight recognizable themes."

Its unearthly song varies in pitch and throbs like a beating

AL GIDDINGS/IMAGES UNLIMITED INC.

DES & JEN BARTLETT

latitudes to calve in winter. Each calving or breeding ground has its own song. Only the males are known to sing, and each year's popular score is known to every male humpback in the area. This fact leads scientists to believe that the mysterious music is an aspect of courtship, along with aggressive male behavior. "If so," says Payne, "humpback bulls are like warriors of old, who had to demonstrate skill in the arts as well as with the sword to win their ladies."

For 30 years the Society's Committee for Research and Exploration has funded dozens of whale research projects. Few findings have been as fascinating as those reported by Roger and Katy Payne (above), whose studies of humpback songs revealed intriguing information about the lives of humpback whales and inspired many human musicians.

Their work with the endangered humpbacks has greatly advanced our appreciation for these rare virtuosos that keep the seas alive with the sound of music.

drum. Unlike other species of singing whales, the humpback is a composer that constantly tinkers with its song. The song may change completely in just a few years.

Humpbacks migrate to temperate and polar latitudes to feed during summer and toward tropical

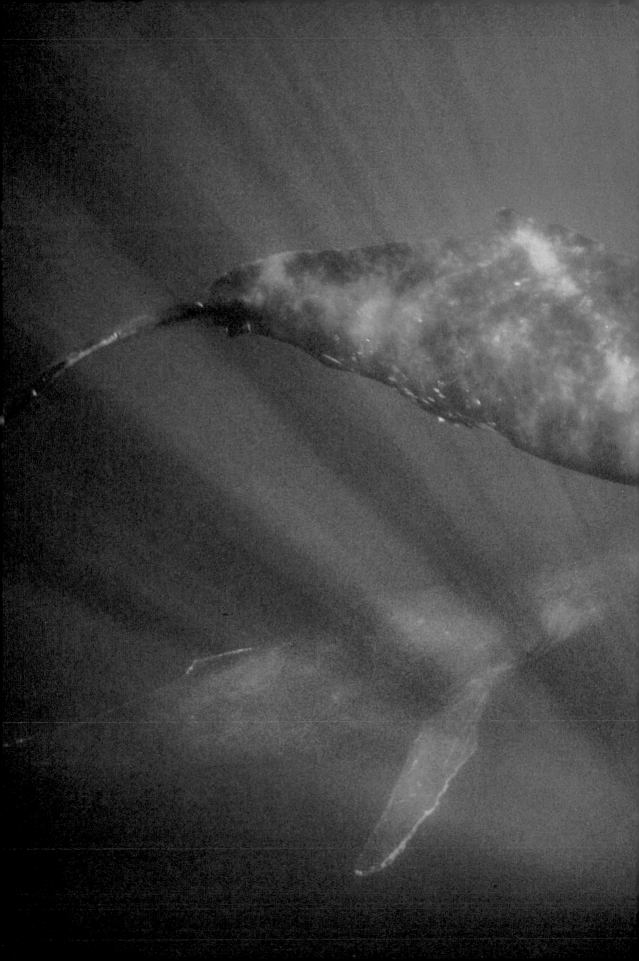

Two humpback whales glide in the
sunlit sea off Hawaii. Huge tail flukes
and flippers as long as 15 feet propel
the nomadic behemoths, which roam
in all the world's oceans.

Canadian sea ice supports the camp of a 1983 Society-backed expedition exploring the *Breadalbane*. The British bark holds title as the northernmost shipwreck ever discovered.

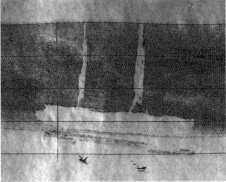

Ghostly side-scan sonar image reveals the first glimpse of the *Breadalbane* in more than a century. Nearly intact, she sits upright on the bottom in 340 feet of numbing Arctic water.

siphonophores, kin to Portuguese men-of-war. Also active in the benthic black were archaeobacteria, among the most ancient life-forms. They may have been some of the first organisms to appear on earth, three to four billion years ago.

So many primitive species in one place. Why? Are hot vents at the bottom of the sea gateways to the origin of life on earth? Some scientists think so.

From this murky kingdom *Alvin* ascended to praise. "The camera performed beyond our best expectations, obtaining close-up color footage of the animal life," Ballard reported. From the CCD's videotape came the Emmy award-winning National Geographic Special, "Dive to the Edge of Creation."

Known as WASP for the insect it resembles, a high-tech suit encases a diver recovering the wheel of the *Breadalbane*. Space-age tools enabled divers to reach the ship at last.

Hot-vent exploration stimulated development of manned submersibles and the birth of small, tethered robotic-computer-camera packages known as remotely operated vehicles (ROVs). Manned submersibles outfitted with advanced technology enabled scientists to probe the largest undersea geyser field yet recorded. It forms a mound the size of Houston's Astrodome in a valley of the Mid-Atlantic Ridge—part of the earth's longest mountain range. Its discovery convinced skeptics that hydrothermal springs occur outside the volcanically active Pacific.

The first extensive study of the ridge's submarine geography stems from Society grants bestowed on geologist Maurice Ewing in the late 1940s. Ewing worked under sail from the deck of the research vessel *Atlantis*. "Behind the ship we towed what we called 'the fish,' a magnetometer that recorded changes in the magnetism of the rocks on the bottom far below, the first time this had been done in the ocean basins," Ewing wrote. "Probably the whole ridge is highly volcanic."

He was on to something. The Mid-Atlantic Ridge is a wild landscape of volcanic mountains laced with magma-heated springs. Years later, in the seventies and eighties, scientists in submersibles hovered near the magma furnaces along the ridge. Their reports confirmed Ewing's suspicions.

Fountains in the Sea

On the Pacific floor, "smoke" from a crusty chimney flags a widening rift, where two of the earth's crustal plates pull apart a few centimeters a year.

As the plates separate, volcanic and hydrothermal activity continually ruptures the rift's thin mantle. Through the fissures pour dark clouds of minerals pressure-cooked by the earth's fiery core. When the heated fluid strikes cold seawater, iron, zinc, and other minerals precipitate, building mineral "chimneys" and blanketing the area with metallic sediments.

These hot vents, known as "black smokers," are found along the Mid-Ocean Ridge. Wrapped around the earth like a rocky seam, the ridge is the world's largest and most volcanically active chain of mountains. The thunderous rumblings and spewing fountains occur in the ocean depths, which until recent years defied accurate mapping of the ridge.

The Society gained a lead in defining the segment of the system known as the Mid-Atlantic Ridge. Grants to Maurice Ewing in the 1940s launched the first geological survey of these submerged peaks and valleys. Thirty years later, the first manned dives to the ridge confirmed Ewing's hunch that the Atlantic's mountainous seafloor was born of fire.

Through grants, and by providing cameras, film, and photographic experts, the Society has greatly extended scientists' ability to see and record phenomena in the abyss.

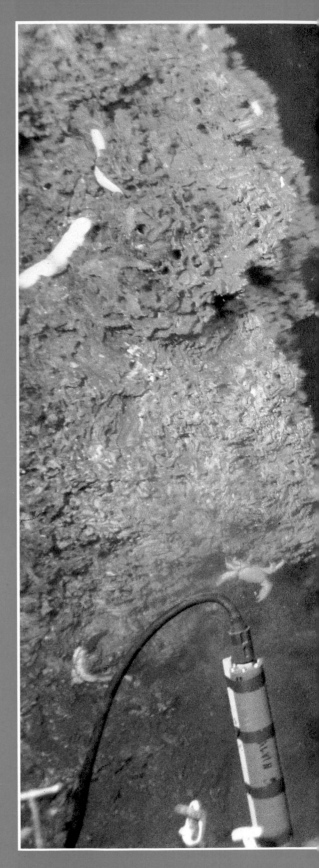

DUDLEY B. FOSTER

Do Edens of creation hide other secrets in the pitch darkness of the Mid-Atlantic's deep? In search of answers, recent Society grants have sent scientists back down to the ridge for further study.

Meanwhile, remotely operated vehicles have cast light on freshwater vents too. A Society-sponsored ROV probing Siberia's Lake Baikal in 1990 flashed images of heated springs pouring from a tectonically active rift. Never before had hot vents been seen in a freshwater area. The finding strongly suggests that Lake Baikal is a new ocean in the making.

ROVs have also distinguished themselves in undersea archaeology. A Geographic-funded robotic conducted the first ROV photo survey of a sunken vessel, H.M.S. *Breadalbane*, which lies in 340 feet of Canadian Arctic water.

This century's most famous shipwreck, R.M.S. *Titanic*, was found by *Argo*, a highly sensitive camera sled that took shape at Woods Hole with Geographic assistance. *Argo* located it in 1985, more than two miles down in the North Atlantic—the first sighting of the ship since it sank 73 years earlier.

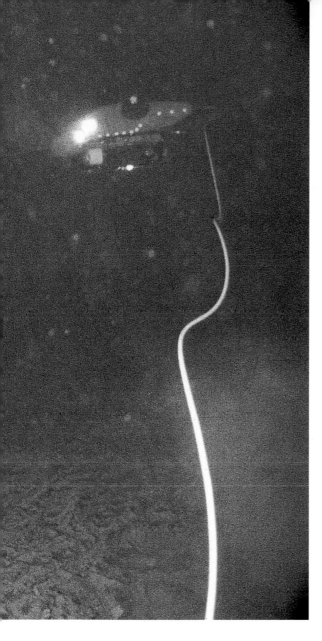

Tethered robot *Jason Jr.* surveys
the hull of the 20th century's most
storied shipwreck, R.M.S. *Titanic*.
Above, *Jason* is controlled from
a console in the famed submersible
Alvin, manned here by Robert Ballard
(on the radio) and pilot Dudley Foster.
Argo, a highly sensitive camera sled
funded in part by Geographic grants,
helped find the ill-fated passenger
liner, which lay buried for seven
decades in the North Atlantic's gloom.

Combining high-tech savvy with
old-fashioned fish bait, noted ichthyologist Eugenie Clark turns the manned
submersible back to basics. She uses it as
a blind for observing and photograph-
ing sea life.

"We set out bait and wait quietly
with the submersible settled on the bottom," Dr. Clark explained. The sub's
thallium iodide lamps bathe the bait
cage in a moonglow, dim enough not to
scare fish but bright enough to see them.

"Ever since I was a child I wanted to
be like William Beebe, the first biologist
to see and describe deep-sea animals,"
Dr. Clark said. She more than fulfilled
her dream in the Beebe Project, an on-
going study of undersea life backed by
Society grants.

Starting in 1987, she bested Beebe's
dives off Bermuda. She stationed her
bait-and-lens submersible more than a
mile below the surface and drew local
residents in close for natural portraits.
Among them was a huge sixgill, a shark
rarely seen in its habitat by humans.

Encouraged by the results and additional Society help, Dr. Clark set out for

Somnolent Sharks

As docile as a sleeping dog, a
man-eating shark lies motionless in
an undersea grotto, contradicting
the theory that sharks need to move
constantly to breathe.

In the 1970s, "sleeping" sharks
represented a perplexing mystery.
Why would one of nature's most
skilled predators, with practically
no natural enemies, take time out
to "hide" in a cave?

To try to find the answer, noted
ichthyologist Eugenie Clark secured
a Society grant and, with additional
funding, led several expeditions to
the only known places where reef
sharks are regularly found in a
sleeplike state—the caves of La
Punta, El Puente, and La Cadena
off the Yucatán Peninsula.

Dr. Clark found the sharks to be
more in a drugged daze than asleep.
Fresh water seeping into the caves
and mingling with salt water cre-
ates an electromagnetic field, and
sharks exposed to this phenomenon
may get "high" and lethargic, much
as humans are affected by alcohol.

The high oxygen content of the
cave water may encourage a shark
to rest quietly, pumping water over
its gills for hours on end. The
water's lower-than-normal salinity
weakens the grip of parasites, making them easier for a remora, a type
of shark sucker, to remove.

"It seems quite likely to me,"
Dr. Clark notes, "that our 'sleeping'
sharks are drawn into the caves
first to get cleaned and second to
enjoy a 'high' of pleasant sensa-
tions. Between the remoras and possible chemical cleansing, the big
fish are kept sleek and spotless."

Japan two years later. Daring dives in Suruga Bay carried her far below the reflection of Mount Fuji. Four thousand feet down, her research team filmed the largest animal ever seen in the deep, a Pacific sleeper shark.

"It was truly a deep-sea monster, at least 23 feet long," Dr. Clark related. "We know sharks perform a vital service. They help keep the ocean healthy by

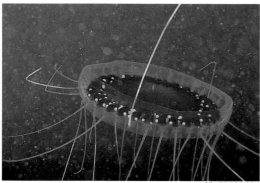

Alien in the abyss, a remotely operated vehicle (ROV) encounters a *Metridium* anemone. At depths below 500 feet, a realm once considered barren, submersibles have revealed a world of creatures, such as the ten-inch-wide narcomedusa (above).

preying on sick and injured fish. But how deep do sharks go and how big do they get?

"The bizarre and grotesque shapes of deep-sea fishes stir the imagination," she said. "Understanding these creatures and their role in a complex global food web could solve many mysteries."

Dr. Clark paused, then added, "Our entire living planet ultimately depends on the ocean's life-forms, but we're just beginning to understand them."

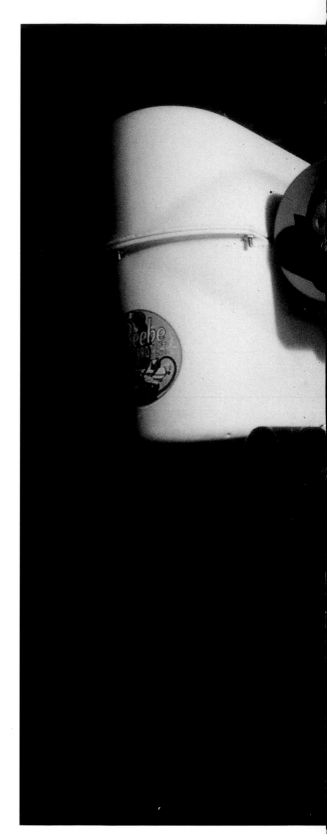

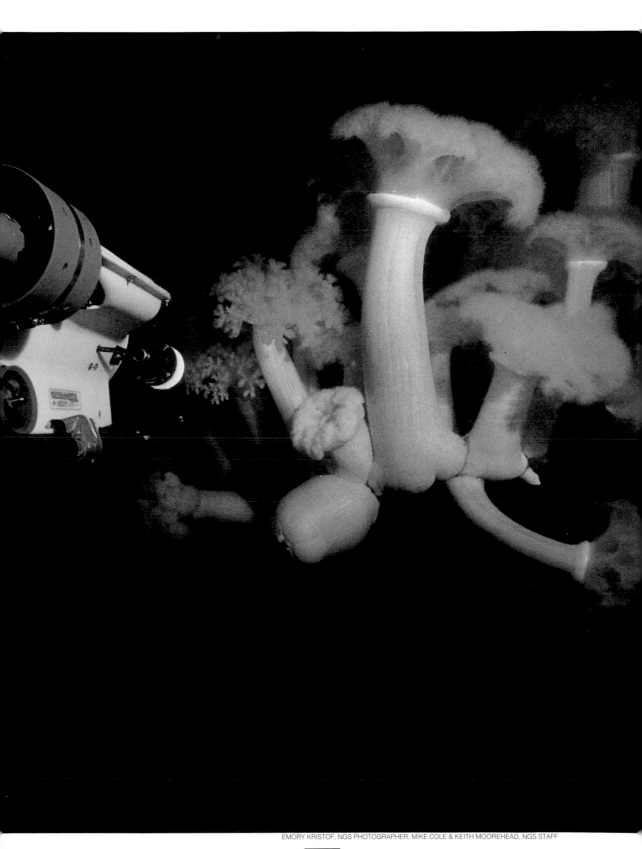

The Future

By Ron Fisher

very National Geographic research grant is a small piece of an enormous puzzle, a minute answer to big questions: Who are we? Where did we come from? Where are we going? What makes our planet tick?

Blazing corona (opposite) reveals secrets of solar energy during a 1991 eclipse. NGS funds and special filters helped map the sun's temperatures.

Preceding Pages: Grantee Cathy Langtimm aims a shotgun microphone at denizens of a Costa Rican rain forest. She may overhear the *zeet zeet zeet* of poison-arrow frogs (above).

Gradually, but as surely as time and tide, science accumulates the findings that make our world comprehensible, and Society grants are a part of the engine that makes science go.

In the past, the Committee for Re-search and Exploration has funded projects in a broad range of disciplines, including anthropology, biology, geography, geology, paleontology, oceanography, and volcanology.

But what of the future?

In 1988, at a symposium of scientists celebrating the centennial of the Society, President Gilbert M. Grosvenor summarized its past exploits and said, "Now explorers are turning more and more to new priorities—the exploration of escalating problems that affect the quality of life on this planet. And while the 20th century will be remembered as an era of extraordinary advances in science, technology, communication, and transportation, I suspect that the 21st century will be chronicled as a period of grappling with global and ecological equilibrium, the depletion of traditional natural resources, and maintaining a stable world population."

Though as puzzling as ever, the world is a smaller place now. Probably there are few Machu Picchus left to be found.

Barry C. Bishop, vice president for research and exploration at the Society, chairs the committee. "Tomorrow's grants will stress somewhat different areas than in the past. We'll be reintroducing the concept of scientific exploration—principally through grants that harness high technology. There are three areas we think really important for future research: the 70 percent of the earth's surface that lies beneath the sea; second, exploring earth from space; and third, biodiversity.

"We hope, too, to be on the cutting edge of research that is reflective of 'change' in our world, and those issues

that directly or indirectly affect the quality of life.

"We are now taking some initiatives beyond our normal grant program. In 1992, we signed a memorandum of agreement with the U.S. Geological Survey to work on freshwater issues. We are also collaborating closely with the Environmental Protection Agency and the National Science Foundation. We'll also be looking for more ways to cooperate with scientists in other countries. We believe the days of 'academic imperialism' are over—when scientists would simply descend on a country, do their research, then leave.

"Among the foreign scientists we are working with are the Russians, with whom we have a project to study Siberian tigers." The Siberian tiger, the world's largest cat, may weigh 600 pounds. There are only a few hundred

TED SPIEGEL/BLACK STAR

remaining in the wild, largely in the Sikhote-Alin Biosphere Reserve about 400 miles north of Vladivostok. Poachers prey on the animals for their pelts and bones and body parts, which are used in Asian folk medicines. The breakup of the Soviet Union and the resulting economic chaos, opening of borders, and the letting of large timber concessions have combined to threaten the tigers' habitat. Russian and American scien-

Air pollution: Industrial pollutants darken the Arizona sky. Concern for our planet is leading to more studies of such environmental hazards.

tists, funded in part by the Geographic, are trying to find out what sort of environment the tigers need to survive.

An American-Chinese expedition in 1992 was also partly funded by NGS. Scientists retrieved ice cores from a

New technology: Humanity's heavy hand shows in Landsat images of the same terrain taken 11 years apart—a Brazilian rain forest scarred by tracks made as settlers cleared the trees.

glacier on the Tibetan Plateau that may reveal climate going back 200,000 years.

A grant in 1993 to Carol P. Harden of the Department of Geography at the University of Tennessee represents a new way to look at an old subject: rain forests. Her study: "Trails, Soil Erosion, and Ecotourism in the Tropical Rainforest." Though ecotourism is generally considered a good thing, severe erosion has been associated with tourist paths in the tropics, but no scientific studies have previously monitored or documented the erosional impact.

Recently AIDS became a subject for consideration by the committee. With a 1993 grant, Priscilla C. Reining of the University of Florida is studying the sustainability of the human, plant, and animal resources of Haya villages in Tanzania as they are affected both by rapid population growth and by increasing incidence of HIV/AIDS.

Future grants will doubtless focus on areas traditionally of interest to the Geographic—land, sea, and sky—but will probably reflect changes in all fields. In archaeology, according to Geographic staff archaeologist George E. Stuart, several exciting new techniques and areas of interest will receive support from the committee. "Blood chemistry and the tracking of DNA, which can both be done from ancient skeletons, will provide information on the diet of ancient peoples, for instance, and on their relationships and migration patterns.

"The way we study sites is changing as well. Satellite imagery—not just photographs, but things like temperature and the geologic character of the land—will help us better understand the

Overpopulation: On a holy day in Bombay, India, an explosion of citizens immerses images of gods in the Arabian Sea. Some neighborhoods squeeze 2,000 people onto each acre.

ancient characteristics of a landscape. And when we're able to see through the canopy of trees by satellite...we'll be able to save a lot of time in the mapping of sites, especially surface features like walls and crumbled structures.

"The conservation of sites is another area that will receive attention. High-tech satellite imaging may allow us to analyze sites without so much digging, which would be a good thing."

Other areas of research that the committee has supported will change in similar ways and just as dramatically. In the search for evidence of early man, for instance, high-tech advances in the study of geology may receive support. Images from satellites will allow researchers to plot strata where fossils have been found, and, perhaps as important, provide negative evidence by iso-

lating areas where they know fossils will *not* be found.

In the study of animals, the Craighead brothers gave up their youthful adventurousness for more advanced forms of tracking—by heat-sensing devices, for example, or by satellite. Grizzlies will be wrestled metaphorically more often than physically. Future research will help sort out the various causes for the demise of species—which declines are induced by natural forces, for instance, and which by humans, with their pollution and otherwise altered ecosystems.

Frank C. Whitmore, Jr., vice chairman of the committee and retired USGS research geologist, says, "The committee, being mostly scientists, is geared toward the specific and the well organized, and we're facing problems that

International cooperation: Grantee Howard Quigley, in a joint research project with the Russians, checks the radio collar on a sedated Siberian tiger, largest of the world's cats.

HOWARD B. QUIGLEY

are *not* specific and well organized. And that's life.

"We are more elastic than most granting agencies. I like that about the Geographic—its willingness to judge each application on its own merits. Once in a while the question is raised: Is this geography? Or, What is the geographic aspect of this grant request? Everything is a continuum, but the continuum is full of gaps. Someone will say, 'Nobody knows anything about X in X area, and this looks like a way to give it a whirl.'

"I'm also proud of our willingness to support beginning researchers. In the last few years we've even awarded grants to graduate students, though we only do that when we're satisfied that the student is already a freestanding researcher and a self-starter."

In March 1993, the Society's 5,000th research grant was awarded—to a young woman studying chimpanzees in Africa. Appropriately for such a milestone grant, Rosalind Alp, in the tradition of Jane Goodall, has taken as her subject the behavioral ecology of a community of wild chimpanzees in the Tambara Hills of Sierra Leone. So the torch is being passed.

Bmut such grants, which involve exciting and even dangerous field research, are increasingly rare. Barry Bishop remembers fondly the old days, when a lone researcher, far from home, pestered by dust, sweat, and bugs, lived an adventure. Now, as more and more field research requires computer analysis of data, for instance, or

186

Lasers in a caldera at Long Valley, California, measure minute changes in the landscape. Mirrors reflect the beams; transit time records movement of the earth's plates.

sophisticated dating techniques, the committee must increasingly make grants for those purposes. Bishop hopes, however, that NGS will always focus primarily on field research. "We are a committee for research *and* exploration," he says. "Field research is an exploration, an adventure, and—to succeed—must be a personal passion as well."

About 80 percent of all Society grants have been awarded since 1980. Nearly half the grant applications considered are approved; in 1992, the committee considered 522 applications and approved 250. The average grant was $14,000, from a budget that year of about $3,500,000. Grants for multi-year projects are most often allocated incrementally, with each year's award contingent upon a written interim report.

Grantees are encouraged to publish their findings in scholarly journals; some appear in *Research & Exploration*, a scientific journal published quarterly by the Society since 1985.

The committee meets monthly to discuss proposals and to make recommendations regarding funding. Over the decades, some of the country's most distinguished scientists, including Robert F. Griggs, Matthew L. Stirling, and Leonard Carmichael, have served on it.

The committee prides itself on providing hassle-free grants. Field biologist George Schaller says, "The Geographic is one of the very few organizations that give money quickly and without too many strings attached. If you go to some other agencies, you've got to spend a month writing a proposal, and then the chances are only one in ten at best that you'll get the money."

Spectacular but deadly, lava from Sicily's Mount Etna sweeps all before it. Scientists hope to improve volcano monitoring to eliminate the risk of surprise eruptions.

Rain forests hold myriad scientific secrets, which are lost as trees are cleared. Forester Frank Miller (above) hoists a Global Positioning System so a satellite can pinpoint his location.

An anecdote from the not-too-distant past illustrates how informally fund requests were once handled—and how times have changed.

One day in 1976, Ivor Noël Hume, who was supervising the archaeological work at Wolstenholme Towne seven miles from Colonial Williamsburg, received a call from the head of the Williamsburg Foundation, Carlisle H. Humelsine. It seems that Melville Bell Grosvenor (MBG to his colleagues), the chairman of the National Geographic Society, was in town, and Humelsine wondered if Noël Hume was doing anything that might interest him. Though

LAUREN GREENFIELD; LARRY ULRICH (OPPOSITE AND FOLLOWING PAGES)

then in his mid-seventies, MBG had a still-boyish enthusiasm for the world and everything in it and was ever eager to learn about new things.

Noël Hume met with MBG, showed him some slides, and told him about the work they had done and about an elusive kiln they were looking for. "Although he was hearing the name Wolstenholme Towne for the first time," wrote Noël Hume, "he stopped me now and again to ask pertinent questions that made me feel that he had been involved with the project at least as long as I had. But when I was through, he said nothing."

Noël Hume made small talk. More silence. "But as I passed him to turn up the lights, the old man put out his hand to stop me.

" 'You ought to find that kiln, you know.'"

MBG asked about the size of the current budget. "We'd contribute part of next year's costs, if that's what you need to keep going," he said. "You shouldn't give up until you've found your kiln." As it turned out, they never did find it. And today grants are awarded with a good deal more care and formality.

But the search for the kiln was as important as the kiln itself. The search is what science is all about, and the spirit that kept Noël Hume and his team looking—and the spirit that made MBG want to help—is the same that has kept the National Geographic Society avidly unlocking the world's secrets for more than a hundred years.

Sunset burnishes the still waters of Everglades National Park. Perhaps the world's most precious commodity, fresh water faces threats everywhere. As part of the Society's water initiative, experts cataloged the most critical issues, and the committee authorized $350,000 in 10 projects to study them.

Recipients of the National Geographic Society's Centennial Awards in November 1988 flank President Gilbert M. Grosvenor: (seated, from left) George F. Bass, Harold E. Edgerton, Jacques-Yves Cousteau, Barbara Washburn, Mary D. Leakey, Frank C. Craighead, Jr., and John J. Craighead; (standing, from left) Sen. John Glenn, Robert D. Ballard, Kenan T. Erim, Bradford Washburn, Jane Goodall, Richard E. Leakey, Thayer Soule, and Sir Edmund Hillary.

Notes on the Authors

While on the Society's staff, **LESLIE ALLEN** wrote *Liberty: The Statue and the American Dream* for the Statue of Liberty-Ellis Island Foundation, and chapters in many NGS books. She now free-lances for the *New York Times* and other publications.

Staff writer **RON FISHER** has written extensively—on diverse subjects for both adults and children—for the Society's book divisions during his career, which now exceeds 30 years. His most recent book is about the Blue Ridge Mountains.

JENNIFER C. URQUHART, on the National Geographic staff since 1971, has contributed to numerous Special Publications, including *The Emerald Realm,* which took her to gorilla country in West Africa. She also explored bison territory for *America's Hidden Treasures: Exploring Our Little-Known National Parks.*

SEYMOUR L. FISHBEIN, retired writer-editor of National Geographic books, was the author of the Special Publications *Grand Canyon Country* and *Yellowstone Country.* He recently contributed a chapter about Voyageurs National Park to *America's Hidden Treasures.*

RICHARD M. CRUM was a co-author of the Society's first Special Publication about the ocean, *World Beneath the Sea.* Writer, editor, and teacher, he has been contributing to Geographic publications since 1964.

Acknowledgments

The Book Division wishes to thank the many grant recipients who provided invaluable help. We are also grateful to Barry C. Bishop, Chairman of the Committee for Research and Exploration; Mary G. Smith, senior assistant editor for research grant projects; and George E. Stuart, senior assistant editor for archaeology.

Additional Reading

The reader may wish to consult the *National Geographic Index* for related articles and books. The following books may also be of interest:
C. D. B. Bryan, *The National Geographic Society: 100 Years of Adventure and Discovery.* Donald Johanson and James Shreeve, *Lucy's Child: The Discovery of a Human Ancestor;* Richard Leakey, *Origins Reconsidered.* Sylvio Acatos, *Pueblos: Prehistoric Indian Cultures of the Southwest;* George F. Bass, *Archaeology Beneath the Sea: A Personal Account;* Joseph Jay Deiss, *Herculaneum: Italy's Buried Treasure;* Melvyn C. Goldstein and Cynthia M. Beall, *Nomads of Western Tibet: The Survival of a Way of Life;* M. Inez Hilger, *Together with the Ainu: A Vanishing People;* Sidney D. Kirkpatrick, *Lords of Sipan: A True Story of Pre-Inca Tombs, Archaeology, and Crime.* Jane Goodall, *In the Shadow of Man; Through A Window: My Thirty Years with the Chimpanzees of Gombe;* and *Chimpanzee Family Book;* L. David Mech, *The Arctic Wolf: Living With the Pack;* George B. Schaller, *Stones of Silence: Journeys in the Himalaya* and *The Last Panda;* Shirley Strum, *Almost Human;* Merlin Tuttle, *America's Neighborhood Bats* and *Batman: Exploring the World of Bats.* Frank C. Craighead, *Track of the Grizzly;* Joan Dunning, *The Loon: Voice of the Wilderness;* Tom Klein, *Loon Magic;* Judith W. McIntyre, *The Common Loon: Spirit of the Northern Lakes;* Alan F. Poole, *Ospreys: A Natural and Unnatural History;* Fred A. Urquhart, *The Monarch Butterfly: International Traveler.* Jacques Cousteau, *Men Under Water;* Victoria A. Kaharl, *Water Baby: The Story of Alvin.*

The Committee for Research and Exploration

The National Geographic Society, through the Committee for Research and Exploration, offers grants-in-aid for basic, original, scientific field research and exploration covering a broad spectrum of disciplines from anthropology to zoology. Particular emphasis is placed on multidisciplinary environmental projects.

Investigators with advanced degrees (Ph.D. or equivalent) and associated with institutions of higher learning or other scientific and educational nonprofit organizations or museums are eligible to apply. Only occasionally are grants awarded to exceptionally well-qualified graduate students with well-established publications records, or to scientific researchers without advanced degrees.

Applications may be submitted at any time. Applicants should allow at least eight months between the date an application is received and the date the committee decides. Inquiries may be addressed to:
Steven S. Stettes, Secretary
Committee for Research and Exploration
National Geographic Society
1145 17th Street, N.W.
Washington, D.C. 20036-4688

Index

Boldface indicates illustrations.

Library of Congress CIP data

Unlocking secrets of the unknown with National Geographic / prepared by the Book Division, National Geographic Society, Washington, D. C.
    p.   cm.
    Includes index.
    ISBN 0-87044-908-7
    1. Geography—Research. 2. National Geographic Society (U.S.)
I. National Geographic Society (U.S.). Book Division.
G73.U49 1993
910'.9—dc20   93-27590
                                                     CIP

Composition for this book by the National Geographic Society Book Division with the assistance of the Typographic section of National Geographic Production Services, Pre-Press Division. Set in Palatino. Printed and bound by R. R. Donnelley & Sons, Willard, Ohio. Color separations by Graphic Art Service, Inc., Nashville, Tenn.; Lanman Progressive Co., Washington, D.C.; Lincoln Graphics, Inc., Cherry Hill, N.J.; and Phototype Color Graphics, Pennsauken, N.J.; Dust jacket printed by Miken Systems, Inc., Cheektowaga, N.Y.